ASANTE CHILDREN'S THEATRE

WORD DANCE

·2018·

Edited by Barbara Shoup

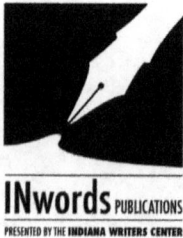

Asante Children's Theatre: WORD DANCE: 2018
ISBN: 978-0-9967438-8-4
INwords Publications, Indianapolis, IN
Printed in the United States of America

INwords PUBLICATIONS
PRESENTED BY THE INDIANA WRITERS CENTER

ASANTE CHILDREN'S THEATRE
WORD DANCE
2018

Edited by Barbara Shoup
Designed by Andrea Boucher, AB Book Designs

INwords Publications
1125 Brookside Avenue, Suite B25
Indianapolis, IN 46202

with special thanks to

An Anonymous Fund of the Central Indiana Community Foundation

additional support from

TABLE OF CONTENTS

A WORD OF THANKS

To an Anonymous Fund of the Central Indiana Community Foundation.

To the Indiana Writers Center's Executive Director, Barbara Shoup, for invaluable input and to IWC Board President, Celeste Williams for sharing in the experience.

To Joanna Taft, CEO at The Harrison Center, for recognizing how powerful and necessary this project was.

To the amazing guest writers who had no idea of what to expect but clearly enjoyed working with a room of people who looked like them but had different histories and were of various ages and gender. Kudos to Allyson Horton, Maurice Broaddus, Ashley Mack-Jackson of Word As Bond, Mitchell L. H. Douglas, Dylan Pritchett, and Deborah Asante. It was your unique style of sharing and words of encouragement that inspired the confidence to produce this remarkable literary work.

To our Families, whose enthusiasm and commitment enriched this unprecedented achievement.

And finally, to Deborah Asante and Keesha Dixon, Founding Artistic Director and Executive Director of The Asante Children's Theatre respectively, who believed in and worked tirelessly to move "WORD DANCE: The Literary Arts Initiative" from conceptualization to reality. Job well done EVERYONE!

WORD DANCE: The Family Literary Project was conceived and managed by Keesha Dixon.

WORD DANCE: THE FAMILY WRITING PROJECT

For nearly thirty years, the Asante Children's Theatre (ACT) has been a beacon of light and a place of solace for young people in search of direction, inspiration and affirmation. Founded by Deborah Asante in 1990, ACT stands firm as a cultural leader in the Indianapolis arts community. Through the performing arts, ACT creates legitimate life-changing experiences for the racially marginalized families it works with. In this way, ACT advances its mission to use the arts to strengthen life-skills in youth.

Among young people are potential artists, writers, philosophers and entrepreneurs. Carter G. Woodson, the "Father of the Black History Month" believed that Blacks should be proud of their heritage and that other Americans should also understand it.

There is a need for young people to develop their authentic voices and not just through performance art. In response to that need, ACT constructed a stand-alone creative writing component for families to cultivate interest in the African and African American experience. The "WORD DANCE Literary Arts Initiative" was an experiment and became the canopy under which ACT would launch two new programs: "The Family Writing Project" and "Tellin' Family Stories."

ACT partnered with The Indiana Writers Center (IWC) because of IWC's mission to support Indiana writers of all ages and backgrounds. IWC coordinated African American workshop facilitators who had very diverse writing styles and identified a designer for the print anthology. The Harrison Center provided affordable artistic space. ACT eagerly promoted the project to its audience, hoping to recruit twenty-five participants who would agree to meet once a week for thirteen weeks to eat, talk and write together.

Consistently, at each weekly session, twenty-one individuals representing eight families had a chance to eat a meal together—time to relax, tell stories, laugh, recharge and bond as family. These families were receptive and enthusiastic about sharing the richness of their life experiences through this creative process where there was clearly a cultural connection to the "professional" writers. This was a great motivation for the young writers whose growing confidence electrified the elder members of the class.

This book represents the zenith of "WORD DANCE: The Family Writing Project." It symbolizes what is possible when barriers are removed and we overlook differences, whether they are age, gender, race or religion. It epitomizes the essence of our similarities. And finally, it preserves the singular and collective reactions to those special moments in our lives. I encourage you to take it all in.

—Keesha Dixon
Executive Director, Asante Children's Theatre

DEDICATION

WORD DANCE is dedicated to Diane Lewis. This gesture is meant to honor her memory, acknowledge her contribution, and add to her legacy. She was an award-winning poet, yet she was so much more to all of us at the Asante Children's Theatre.

Our Executive Director, Keesha Dixon, recognized in her friend, Diane, rare and wonderful qualities and talked her into volunteering with ACT in 1999. It quickly became apparent that Diane Lewis was what I call a puzzle piece, someone who completes the picture. She joined our staff, first as Executive Administrative Assistant, then going on to head her own department as Volunteer Coordinator. Her insightful work with volunteers helped to strengthen our organization beyond measure.

Diane always had a keen sense of what was needed and she would step in to get it done. Her poetic sensibilities often led her to offer the right word or pose a significant question that could help you turn the corner on an important project. Her trademark was gentleness. Her kindness and generosity could be counted upon. Her dedication was a gift. Her sense of humor, quirky, and her laugh, infectious. Oh, how she is missed.

Diane was a creative force in her own right and she used her artistic might to help build and better the Asante Children's Theatre and the talents of the young artists who tumbled through our doors. We were blessed to have her ideas and dreams stirred into all things Asante.

—**Deborah Asante**
Founder/Artistic Director, Asante Children's Theatre

When We Are Among Children

Diane Lewis

···❀···

When we are among children,
especially the little ones, the noisy ones,
the ones with runny noses and sticky fingers,
we can discover a thousand beams of light
giving off hints of happiness

Even the gloomy despair of a forgotten life
is chased away by children.

I would almost say that they save us.
Can we deny their innocent power
or their perfect intent?

They bring us back from
the daily crush of life,
beckoning us to the sandbox,
inviting us out to play,
urging us to stay awhile
when we are among children.

Diane Lewis

Asante Family

Terrance's First Word

Deborah Asante

· · · ✿ · · ·

I COULDN'T WAIT FOR MY baby to talk. His crying always made me nervous because I had to guess what was wrong. We were living in San Francisco in the old Filmore district in a one-bedroom apartment. The place was tiny with big windows facing the north. The walls were white except for the minuscule yellow kitchen. The living room and the bedroom had a red shag carpet. I slept on the couch in the living room and let the baby have the bedroom, in an effort to foster my son's independence.

He would wake me up every morning crying for his bottle. His cry was loud and insistent; of course, I knew what he wanted. It was the other times throughout the day that his cries would confuse me and I would look him in the eyes and say "I wish you could talk to me, I don't understand crying."

Finally, he said his first word, "Mama." The next morning after he spoke that word, he woke up and cried for his bottle. I called from the living room, "Call your Mama and she will bring your bottle." He stopped crying, but after a moment started up again. I repeated my statement "Call your Mama and she will bring your bottle." He stopped crying again and after what felt like a long silence he said, "Mama!" The sweetest sound I've ever heard. I jumped into the room with his morning bottle.

My baby looked a little confused at my entrance but my smile lit his smile. I laughed and so did he as he grabbed his bottle, and as he sucked away on it, his eyes danced with delight. He knew he had done something special. After that Terrance built his vocabulary with gusto and now, as a grown man, my son is one of the strongest communicators I know.

Mother's Day with My Granddaughters

Deborah Asante

· · ·✾· · ·

WE ACTUALLY SPENT THE NIGHT before Mother's Day together. I rented a hotel room because I didn't want the burden of cleaning house before or after our visit and I thought it would make our time together even more special. Staying in a nice hotel always makes me feel luxurious. The Granddaughters have so much power in my life. Just looking at them can make me smile. Seeing things through their eyes always freshens my view. They can also infuriate me with their petty bickering.

I have three sisters and our bond has grown so thick and strong that it has become a treasure I possess. Reminding my girls of the potential value of what they might build together is my constant task.

The girls are currently 8, 10, and 12. Tyla is the eldest. She is tall, lovely and graceful. Her smile lights her way and she never meets a stranger. Charlie comes next and she is the high achiever, with a quick and curious mind. It is important to her to master whatever is set before her. Makenzie, the youngest, is still openly affectionate. Whatever she does, she does with ease, and she is the least concerned with judgement. They all embrace stubbornness, but the two youngest rejoice in it.

We started Mother's Day with breakfast at Cracker Barrel. This was my choice and not theirs, a fact they reminded me of until we were seated for our meal. I curtly reminded them that it was my day as a Mother and Grandmother and we were done discussing it. After that it was smooth sailing. They each crafted me a Mother's day card from the kid's menus. Their creations were immediately revealed as precious gifts. These cards will always bring a rush of how blessed I am and how brief and special these times are.

Sister, Daughter, Mother, Grandmother

Deborah Asante

· · · ✿ · · ·

Sister, daughter, mother, grandmother.
I have spent time as each,
each bitter and sweet
and all too brief.

I have three sisters,
our bond thick and strong.
I have three granddaughters.
May their sticky love
last as long.

Soul Food

Deborah Asante

· · · ✿ · · ·

Soul food, thank God for soul food!
It can answer your hunger, but it also soothes your soul.
Sooooul food, where does it come from?
It must come from love.

Love, passed down generation after generation
from a people who by design
worked from can't see in the morning
'til can't see at night.

Their work filled their days,
broke down their bodies,
and often robbed them of hope.

But a body that works hard
must be a body that's fed.
Out of necessity
weekly food rations were provided.

A peck of corn and
three pounds of fatback or bacon,
some molasses and clabber,
small portions of fruit or vegetables that were in season.

Then from sheer creativity
and the need to share more than hardship,
soul food, comfort food, keep-holding-to-your-hope-food
was born out of those weekly rations.

Those that kept a garden were most fortunate.
Many watched and waited for
what was tossed from the kitchen of the big house.
That overflow from the greedy
found new purpose and flavor
in the hungry pots of the needy.

Cooking was a real way of showing care,
of lavishing love on your family
in a lasting way.

Dishes were created by instinct,
using taste, touch, sight, smell and sound—
like listening to the sizzle and crackle of chicken frying
and knowing from the sound when it was done.

Soul food, soul food.
Sometimes just talking about it
makes me feel good

Buttermilk biscuits & cane syrup,
Grits and fried fish,
Corn fritters, collard greens,
Candied yams, macaroni and cheese,
Oxtails, pig feet, ham and potato salad.
Smothered turkey wings in
my great grandma's gravy brings it all back,

Deborah Asante

makes me remember.
I could thrive on greens, beans and cornbread.
Don't forget the hot sauce!

But life is sweeter with
peach cobbler, caramel cake,
banana pudding & sweet potato pie.

Soul food is love.
Soul food is tradition.
Soul food is survival.

Soul food is my history
wrapped in special recipes and passed down
to strengthen me.

Deborah Asante

Art Is Loving the Task

Deborah Asante

· · · ✿ · · ·

I BELIEVE THAT ART IS loving the task. When you are doing something you truly enjoy and you continue to do it, you become an artist at it. The more you do it, the more you want to do it. When we relax and enjoy ourselves, we become creative and our capacity to problem solve grows big and strong.

Practicing what we love fosters confidence because when we are able to submerge ourselves in a practice, process or activity that is wholly satisfying, we become like children at play. We forget to worry about what others think of us. Our bodies and minds connect to what we seek to achieve and we find purpose. To find purpose elevates our existence.

I believe mathematicians who love math are artists. The biologist that loves the study of biology is an artist. I believe a bicycle repairperson who loves repairing bicycles is an artist. A teacher who loves to teach is an artist. When you love what you do, you find new and different ways of getting it done. You learn to trust your instincts and test the faith you have in yourself. If you are drawn to your work and delight in overcoming its obstacles, you may even become an innovator.

This may sound radical because many of us do what we do out of a sense of duty. We do what is expected of us. We work out of necessity, to pay our bills, to provide for our families. We want the best paying jobs. Most of all we want to be considered successful. However, is that enough if you don't feel like you have connected with your purpose?

What if when you attend school you are actively reminded that it is the place to explore different possibilities? That school is a place to shop for your future. That it is a treasure hunt and you are encouraged to examine each subject, each experience for possible connections to your bliss? The emphasis isn't judging you as a student. Instead the school concentrates on offering diverse samplings and building a curriculum that fosters self-discovery.

A place where students are encouraged to approach all areas of study creatively. Where different styles of learning are embraced and celebrated for the diversity they bring to the educational environment. A place where the standards of success are as varied as the individuals seeking successful outcomes. A place where the love of learning is the dominant culture.

I submit that the perception that only a few of us are gifted enough to live our lives as "artists," loving our work, feeling connected to our purpose is dangerous to the well-being of the whole community.

If art is loving the task, wouldn't it be wonderful if our educational objective was to find the artist in each and every one of us?

Deborah Asante

Bowers Family

To Be a Negro in This Country

Teah Bowers

· · ·❀· · ·

To be a negro in this country and to be relatively conscious is to be in a rage almost all the time...

- On my way to work I heard another story about a black man being shot by the police.
- I heard a story about a black woman being choked and her privates exposed by police.
- I watched a video of a man being slammed on his head and choked until he lost consciousness while one of the police smirked and laughed at him.

All of this in a matter of three days.

I am a negro in this country. I am relatively conscious and I am in a constant rage.

THANK GOD!!! for my husband, for my kids. They are my "CALGON." They take me away from it all. They are my HAPPY PLACE.

Where I'm From

Teah Bowers

· · · ✿ · · ·

I am from playing on the stairs
outside the apartment door.
I'm from Cabbage Patch dresses
and Jelly Bean sandals.
I'm from racing my Daddy to Bethel Park
and him letting me almost win.
I thought I was really fast.

I'm from playing on the stairs
outside our back door, skipping
up the stairs and falling, ending up
with two bloodied knees.
I am from playing games with my cousins
inside the house to running
in the outside garage, bugging
the parents, great aunts and uncles,
and family friends, who are busy playing spades
and Dad, drinking and smoking.

I am from riding with my Daddy around Indy streets
A LOT. That's how I got to know my way around.
I can find my way anywhere, here or out of town.

I'm from science fairs and competition
to 100 Black women meetings, to
basketball games to track meets, to church
to KFC after church every Sunday.

I am from babysitting my baby
sister, hollering at the top of her lungs.
I am from hiding in my bedroom
to avoid my sister.
I am from Aunt Toni's house where
we ate most dinners because my mom
was at school, attaining her teaching degree.
I am riding my bike to Clark's
filling station to get honey buns and
Canadian Mists and Now-and-Laters before
school, hair blowing in the wind.

I am from college tours and
traveling and learning.

I am also from an unknown future.

I'm from working and being a mommy
or at least I was trying to be one.

I am the 80's, 90's, 2000's, 2020's.

Teah Bowers

The Morning of the Boat Trip

Quinton Bowers

· · · ❁ · · ·

THE ALARM GOES OFF AROUND 5:30 a.m., but it seems like it's two in the morning. We have to be at the docks by 7:00 a.m. I call Paul to make sure he is up. Riding there, I cannot think of the last time I've been on a boat. Not sure if my stomach will cooperate or not. Paul says he is cool, but I hear some nervousness in his voice. I know he's scared of bridges, but not quite sure how he'll be on water. When we arrive at the docks, the boat is loaded with men from Love First Christian Church, all shapes and sizes, large and small. I'm starving, but I know I'm prepared with snacks and semi-nervous of being seasick. Before we leave the docks, the captain gets everyone on board on the first level of the boat to go over instructions, answer questions, sign waivers, etc. I'm thinking to myself, thirteen miles does not seem far on land, but on the water it seems endless. I cannot visualize if we could see land at all that far out. After all the talking, the boat takes off and the sound of the engine is churning out. The boat starts to rock vigorously and the look on Paul's face is of intense panic and fear.

Visiting Lolo

Quinton Bowers

$$\cdots \circledast \cdots$$

I HAVE MEMORIES OF MY grandmother but none stand out like those of her sister Lolo...sweet Lolo. I remember like yesterday 3125 Whittier St. Louis Missouri.

"Quinton is that you? Where ya mama and ya daddy going? Dey probably going down to that pool hall down on Natural Bridge. Hears they play good music on Saturday nights. Boy, did you eat dinner?"

"Yes, ma'am. I ate two McDonald's cheeseburgers, fries and a strawberry milkshake."

"Boy, dat ain't no good eatin'. Yeah. Y'all don't know about no good eatin' until you've had a fried tripe sandwich with a little mustard and hot sauce, or even better a St. Paul from the Chinaman down on the corner of Grand. Ahh, that's good eatin', boy. Whatcha know 'bout dat, huh? Yass, dats good eatin'. Wish you was old enough to walk down der and get me one right now...ooh, shole do. Boy, I wish ya grandmama could see you now, she be so proud of you and how big you getting. Ya looking just like to Granddaddy. Go in that kitchen and grab my cigarettes and the coldest Stag beer in the fridge."

Neighborhood

Quinton Bowers

···❀···

3021 COLERAIN DRIVE, MY GRANDPARENTS' house—light colored brick with a mustard yellow trim, on a street tucked in between the heart of Haughville and Marian College. A lot of growing up happened here, from dinners, family reunions, birthdays, and funerals. Happy times and sad times, but the good outweighed the bad. Out front curveball was a neighborhood sport that developed my basketball game. Lofting that basketball to the other side of the street with the perfect amount of touch to get it to bounce back to you. It took skill and persistence, as well as a large amount of guts if you threw it over a moving car for bonus points. Guts, I say, because you never knew what neighbor would immediately pull the car over and tell your parents or grandparents. And the discipline that would follow-up.

It was like a crew of us that were brothers that bonded together. Me, Antwan, Bernie, Derrick, and Leon. Group walks to Atkins Boys Club in the summer were full of adventures filled with alternate routes, sightseeing, pit-stops and over-exaggerated fictitious tales. Long's Donuts...One yeast please. Or having just enough money to pay for an order of crumbs from Long John's Silver, or even lying to Hardee's saying it was your birthday for a free swirl cone. My neighborhood was filled with families and great people.

Mr. Skinner, an old-black man, with a little bit of grey hair atop his head. Drifted into the house with a slow walk once he stepped outside that pearl white Cadillac Fleetwood. Mr. Skinner looked out for me after my grandfather passed away. I remember it like yesterday, walking across the street down two houses, and asking Mr. Skinner if he needed any help. Helping the old people in the neighborhood was a way to get a little extra spare change...One yeast please? Mr. Skinner had a collection of old telephones in the den of his house, and it was like a trip to the museum whenever I took a trip across the street to visit him. He made waffles with this vintage waffle maker that always came out the same way, fluffy and golden brown. Those phones, I always wondered what happened to them. Nowadays, the same buildings still stand, but the faces have mostly changed. But it's my neighborhood.

When I Feel Most at Home

Quinton Bowers

. . . ❁ . . .

Ahh, something about that sweet aroma of charcoal burning takes me to a place.
Oh, what a place.

A mix of Anthony Hamilton and Isley Brothers playing in the background.
Well, well, well.
Oh, what a place

The anticipation is boiling as those jet black coals start to turn snow white.
Ribs, chicken, hot smoked sausage and fresh ears of corn.
Oh, what a place

Time stands still when I'm here, not a worry, not a fear.
I'm at home here.
Cheers, oh, what a place.

Paintings and Art

Tara Bowers

· · · ❦ · · ·

WHEN I GOT HERE TODAY I saw paintings and art, I thought we were drawing. When I came in I figured out that we were writing and eating. I saw more paintings in here. We had cake. I love to paint, it is very creative and fun. I feel like there's art everywhere. There's always family around. When I write I feel courage and happiness.

Buster's Story

WHEN MY NANNA'S DOG DIED he froze in the winter. His name was Buster. He was a little nice dog. I always come to my Nana's house and remember him. And when I see my dog, Bella? I remember him. Every time I went to his house I always pet him. He was a really nice dog. As soon as I heard he died I was sad. And said, "How?" Because I did not know that my Nana and Grandpa left him outside overnight. And then my auntie told me how he died. She lives with them. She helps me remember him because she took pictures of him on her phone. She still has that phone. He was a white and brown dog. He was a rat terrier.

At the Dentist

Tara Bowers

· · · ❁ · · ·

FIRST THEY BRUSHED MY TEETH. Next they scraped stuff off my teeth. It was a sunny day. I watched TV when they did it. They mixed water and air and it tasted really fruity. At the end they gave me a bag with a PINK toothbrush. I don't like pink. I like blue. I gave it to my brother. He likes red and blue.

Cookies

We buy cookies,
we make cookies.
I love cookies,
your great cookies.
Some are soft,
some are hard.
But all cookies taste good.
Cookies are yummy.
I love COOKIES!

Where I'm From

Tara Bowers

· · · ✿ · · ·

I am from Florida,
from the beach,
brown and salty,
from the park,
from the grass.
It feels like water.

I'm from cake pops, sparkly cake pops.
From Daddy, Tasia, Tara, Teah,
Nanna, Ganna, and Grandpa.

I'm from "Be quiet."
I'm from hiding from my mommy and daddy.
I'm from creativity and scrap paper.
I'm from pizza and spaghetti.
I'm from making eggs.

Boxes of toys are under my bed—
baby dolls, Hatchables.

I'm from "Take a nap."

When We Took Tasia to College

Tara Bowers

· · · ❁ · · ·

WE FOUND OUT WHERE HER room was. We found out her roommate. We explored her college. Tasia had to sign stuff. Her roommate's name was Meme. Now the roommate's name is China. We ate at a restaurant and we got mints. When it was dark we left and said bye and went back to Indiana because her college is in Ohio. Her college is Central State.

The Red Transformer and the Zoo

Bryson Bowers

···❁···

THE RED TRANSFORMER IS WORKING on how to drive a car. When he drives he turns into a Transformer car. He drives to the zoo. He sees tigers and elephants.

I like to see the animals when I go to the zoo. I like the horses. I get to ride a brown one.

It feels fun. The horse feels warm and smooth. His back feels super-warm. His name was Bullseye. If you put your hand on the thing on his back, he runs. I said to the horse, "You can run great." He said, "Okay." He speaked in horse.

Florida

WATER IS EVERYWHERE. I PLAY with water at the beach. I build a sandcastle. My daddy helps me. My mom looks for seashells. My sisters find more water for me to put on the sandcastle. The beach is in Florida. I feel happy because one day when I went there I watched shows about hero puppies. I stayed in a hotel.

Where I'm From

Bryson Bowers

···❁···

I am from Florida,
From Indianapolis
and 7811 Blue Willow Drive.
I am from the sand—
brown, warm.
I made a big tall sandcastle.
I am from flowers in the yard
where the grass grows
and tickles my legs.

I'm from purple and pink and red suckers
from my mommy and my sister.
I'm from the video game players
and the TV watchers,
from "Go to sleep and you can watch TV."
I'm from hiding from my daddy and mommy
in their bed with all my toys that I play with.

I'm from me and my daddy,
hot dogs and oranges,
from my hurt knee when I fell
at my Nanna's house
and the finger I hurt with a stick.

Under my bed are my toys.
My Neverland pirate boat,
my Woody, my Tigey,
still when I don't play with them.

I am from Zombieland
where zombies sing and dance.

Bryson Bowers

Black Panther

Bryson Bowers

· · · ❁ · · ·

I DREW SHURI FROM *BLACK PANTHER*. He's my favorite character. I also drew this girl with the bald head and spear. She is my favorite character in the movie. I saw it two times. I'm happy he is still alive. I have an action figure of Killmonger in my room. I really liked the movie. That's why I watched it two times. Also because my Auntie Danielle did not see it.

Taking My Sister to College

T HIS IS MY SISTER. WE'RE driving her to college. It is Central State. It is far away from my house. In the car I watched TV on my mommy's phone. My sister played like she was Oma, the bad pirate. The college looked like a school. It was big. It had snacks in my sister's room. Everybody carried her stuff to her room. I carried her clothes and her favorite food and her book bag. My mom said, "Are you bringing that to your sister?" and I said, "Yes." She has a new friend there. Her name is Danielle. I felt sad when it was time to say goodbye. I said, "Goodbye" and "Good night." My mommy cried. I watched zombies on my mommy's phone on the way home.

Fried Chicken

Bryson Bowers

$$\cdots \circledast \cdots$$

FRIED CHICKEN IS SUPER YUMMY. I like it cause it tastes good. The outside of it is brown. All of the inside is white. I like the outside best because it's crunchy. We get Chicken McNuggets at McDonalds. My daddy cooks barbeque chicken in our backyard. He lets me watch videos while he cooks. I like the boy with the white hair in Descendants Two. We eat at the picnic table. There's mashed potatoes and sweet potatoes for my sister. There's green beans. I like those, too. Also there's salad. We drink lemonade. It tastes sour. I eat one hundred pieces of chicken.

My daddy and my mommy say, "Why are you eating one hundred pieces of chicken?"

"'Cause I want to," I say. I feel good when I am full of fried chicken.

My Neighborhood

Bryson Bowers

· · · ❀ · · ·

MY NEIGHBORHOOD IS BIG AND the grass was growing really high to the sky. There's snow when it's snowing. When I don't know when snow is in the grass, I look out the window. I go outside to see it. I see trees that are growing all the way from the earth to the sky. I see planets moving in the morning.

The people next door have a dog that is little. My dog comes across the gate. I tell my mommy and daddy, "Bella went to our neighbor's house, in the garden," and they yell her name. So she comes back. My favorite thing to do in my neighborhood is a snowball fight with my cousin. I make a big snowball and throw it and try to get it in their face. But I don't. They throw it and get it in my face. Then I get a bigger one.

There's a library in my neighborhood. It has grownup computers, kids' computers, and a lot of books. My nana goes to the library with her students. She teaches them how to read if they don't know how. Working on computers and playing games are my favorite thing at the library. You need a library card to take out books.

When I Feel Most at Home

Bryson Bowers

· · ·✿· · ·

I LIKE MY HOUSE, I walk on my parents backs for massages. I really like getting massages from my sister Tara. The best part is when she walks on my back, and follows up with rubbing lotion on it. She's the best. She is the family massage person. My dad and I always fall asleep. They put us in a happy place.

Briscoe/Briscoe Beuoy Family

Life's Purpose

Mari Briscoe

· · ·❁· · ·

When we are born we become a link in the chain.
Each one is a "part of the continent, a piece of the main."
Everyone is connected, interlocked as mankind.
We are a part of God's purpose, His architectural design.
We are created for a reason and connected to one another
because it's impossible to complete his purpose
without our sisters and brothers.
If one of us falters and stops short of our mission,
it impedes God's plan and dwarfs the coalition.
You see, each one is a stepping stone.
Our purpose is harder to accomplish
without the help of each one.
We're only as "strong as our weakest link."
Our human connectivity is more important than you think.
Imagine your life as a relay race, depending
on the other to pass the baton,
not able to progress until that job is done.
So don't say, it's "my life," because it's bigger than you.
You're an inscriber of destiny, it's not just "yours," but my life too.
Be all you can be and climb the ladder of success.
Give your all and all and do your level best
to accomplish your life's purpose and bring to fruition
by being a positive part of the Human Condition.

Veronique, Mi Amore

Mari Briscoe

· · · ✤ · · ·

When we are born we become a link in the chain.
Each one is a "part of the continent, a piece of the main."
Everyone is connected, interlocked as mankind.
We are a part of God's purpose, His architectural design.
We are created for a reason and connected to one another
because it's impossible to complete his purpose
without our sisters and brothers.
If one of us falters and stops short of our mission,
it impedes God's plan and dwarfs the coalition.
You see, each one is a stepping stone.
Our purpose is harder to accomplish
without the help of each one.
We're only as "strong as our weakest link."
Our human connectivity is more important than you think.
Imagine your life as a relay race, depending
on the other to pass the baton,
not able to progress until that job is done.
So don't say, it's "my life," because it's bigger than you.
You're an inscriber of destiny, it's not just "yours," but my life too.
Be all you can be and climb the ladder of success.
Give your all and all and do your level best
to accomplish your life's purpose and bring to fruition
by being a positive part of the Human Condition.

My Legacy: A Bundle of Joy

Mari Briscoe

· · · ✿ · · ·

A new little angel
arrived just the other day.
She lights up the sky and makes the blue skies stay.
As she smiles at me, my heart goes a flutter.
As far as I'm concerned, there's no perfect other.
Believe it or not, she already giggles,
stands straight on her legs, as her little head wiggles.
Once that's accomplished, she looks at me so proud!
As she talks with her eyes and shouts out loud!
"Look at me, Anais. I'm a big girl, I am!
I'm up on my legs. See how tall I can stand?"
She's growing so fast, by leaps and bounds.
She's my blessed legacy, and earth stands still
whenever she's around. She brings me joy
In the morning and calm in the night.
When I think of her, trouble disappears with
no adversities in sight. She's an extension
of my daughter, who's the love of my life.
I want her future, like her parents', to be brilliant and bright!
The oyster was her vessel and she's that special Black pearl,
doing good things in the future because of her
presence in the world. Oh, yes, there are tremendous

possibilities for this granddaughter of mine.
She'll be gracious and generous, conveying
truth and she'll love all mankind.
She'll not dwell on their heritage, race or ethnic creed.
Just knowing they're God's creation is all she will need.
Her principals will fight for justice, fairness and world peace.
Aspire for no less because my ANAIS.

Dedicated to my granddaughter, Anais

Kui

Mari Briscoe

· · ·✿· · ·

One day I went to volunteer
at the Ronald McDonald House.
A group of us took some books
in the name of
Girl Scouts.
After going about our guided tour,
I came upon some women.
Initially, I didn't say a word,
But then I retraced my beginning route
And blurted out some words.
"May I sit down and have a chat?"
I told them all about me and
Questions I did ask.
They were receptive of my inquiries
and to me they gave their trust.
I had an overwhelming feeling
to care for them I must.
They were in a foreign country,
Lost and all alone,
only having contact
with their loved ones on the phone.
And with them came a little girl

with the most amazing eyes.
I looked at her and instantly
I was mesmerized.
They were large and round
and looked at me as if to hypnotize.
And from that very moment I
Became their friend and guide.
I'd visit them and take them places
and be right by their side.
We'd go to grocery and health food
Stores, to amusement parks and such.
Although I gave myself to them,
they gave me oh so much.
The little girl with magic eyes
was nicknamed Kui.
She loved to look at cartoons and
Play with different toys.
Just hearing and seeing her laugh
And smile
Brought us so much joy.
I bought her once a little toy
whose name was Wanda Weasel.
After playing with it, she'd often sit
And paint upon her easel.
She was sick, then cured, then we rejoiced
and soon began to smile.
Our fervent prayers had been answered
to heal our blessed child.
Her health has since then see-sawed,
but we still have a positive vision
that she'll progress and have success

and we'll honor God's decision.
We'll watch as well as pray
and continue to keep the faith
and know that God gives us only
what we can bear to take.

Dedicated to Natasha "Kui" Wagura
She lost her fight in October, 2007 at eight years old.

Mari Briscoe

Mirror Images

Veronique Briscoe Beuoy

· · ·❀· · ·

She seems familiar
yet somehow completely
unknown

I miss her
or at least who I thought
she'd be

Although there are
just as many days
when remembering
Her naivete
frustrating stubbornness
vision
confidence
blind strength
makes me wish I'd forget

And many other days
when her presence
overwhelms me and

I am grateful
to see her smile
in my reflection

Knowing now
in a way that
I could not have known
then

That thru time
joy
love
pain
distraction

She is sure to
never abandon Me

Veronique Briscoe Beuoy

Life Plan

Veronique Briscoe Beuoy

· · · ❀ · · ·

My life has been
wild and precious
simple and complex
full even when it
has felt empty

Tragic beautiful dream
with nightmare moments

But it has been my own

What is it that I plan to do?

It is no longer about
the What?
It's about the How?

Values

Veronique Briscoe Beuoy

...❁...

Courage
Grace
Simplicity
Synergy
Self-actualization
Playfulness
Love
Abundance
Vitality
Truth

The Sacrifice

Veronique Briscoe Beuoy

· · ·❀· · ·

We are taken for granted

Our beauty
Our strength
Our complexity
The impossibility of ever understanding
How we function
Who we be

You come from us and return to us
Entering our space
Constantly relying on the foreverness
that must lie in the vastness
of our ever varying brown and fertile
Landscape

You commandeer this space
and use the richness of our depths
to create
to control
to expand
to exist
as More

And we yield to you
Your force
Your frustration
Your wanton desire

We wrap ourselves around you
Offering our souls if necessary
To protect you
from yourself
from the external
All that we cannot control
because our entire purpose is to birth you into yourself

Although you have long ago
forgotten
your place in the exchange

Instead
even the best of you
you steal our power
claim it as your own
use our reflections
as evidence
of all that you are capable of
acquiring
possessing
redirecting

And we love you still
even as you lovingly
trample us

Veronique Briscoe Beuoy

sometimes until
we are no longer
recognizable
to ourselves

And we love you still
even as you lovingly
unknowingly
abandon us
to rootless fantasy

And your face
the bewilderment
the fear
as you realize that what
you assumed was forever
was only
a day

Our heart breaks for you
as all that we were
have been
and could be

crumbles under the weight of
you

And
We look at you longingly
loving you still
as we cease to exist

All the Time

Anais Briscoe Beuoy

···❀···

Once upon a time
I was the one who made myself
And
The one who people heard
As I grow in my skin
Sound of Booms
that just keep going on in my head

Anais Briscoe Beuoy

The Do's and Don'ts

Anais Briscoe Beuoy

· · ·✿· · ·

Some who put their heart out
Are not only a fool
But also
a beautiful person

Some who don't put their heart out
are not only scared
But also
Smart

I Am from Me

Anais Briscoe Beuoy

...❀...

I am from
The beautiful whispers of a fox
I am from
My stubborn MiMi and direct mother
I am from
My focused and mature
yet funny and playful aunt
I am from
skinny jeans and gum
pony tails and corn rows and
rollerset hair (I've really only done it once)
I am from
hot tea
peach sherbet and
jasmine rice
I am from
Broccoli and edamame
New pop
Gospel
Hip hop
and a little bit of Jazz
Diaries and Blogs
They are all what I am from!!

Anais Briscoe Beuoy

Once Upon a Time

Anais Briscoe Beuoy

· · ·❀· · ·

ONCE UPON A TIME FAIRY tales did not exist. I know it's sad, but true. Well, that's what I thought at the time. Anyway. I must warn you that if you don't stop reading now I might as well tell you the secret of magic. Oh, no, I've said too much and I can't stop now. I guess I will tell you, but you must swear not to tell anyone, like no one, not even your mom or dad or any of your family and friends, not even your best friend.

Okay. So it all started with a girl named Jade. She was an adventurous girl. That night she went to her room early. She does not know why, but she watched TV for an hour or two, then fell asleep. She woke up at 2 AM to turn the TV off, but she saw a light coming from her closet. So she opened it and there she saw a land. She could tell it was magic. She had read so many books and watched so many movies like this.

So she packed in case it took her awhile. She was prepared. She packed some food, some clothes, and dog food for Button, her dog. She decided to take her, too, so she could protect her and she made her feel good.

She went in and the first thing she saw was a lady. She looked nice, so she went up to say, "Hi."

She replied, "Hello, you're not from here, are you?"

"No," she said quickly.

The lady said, "Well, my name is Kathryn. What is yours?"

"Oh, It's Jade." Then she said, "Where am I?"

Kathryn then said, "Galcoik, Gal-co-ik."

"Galawho?" Jade asked. She knew it would be a weird name, but not that weird.

I Want to Be a Pet

Anais Briscoe Beuoy

. . . ✿ . . .

I'M A COCKROACH, BUT I want to be a pet. Well, me and my sister do. To be fed every morning and night, to be loved and cared for would be a dream come true.

Oh, I'm so sorry. I forgot to introduce my sister and me. Well, my name is Chirper and my sister's name is Princess. Yes, I know Princess is not fit for a nasty bug. Well, guess what? We don't care one bit about what you think.

Now it's time for me and my sis to try one more time to be a pet. Wish us luck.

Stop Bullying!

Kwalli Fox-Briscoe

· · · ✿ · · ·

THERE WAS A TIME WHEN me and my friends made a slide about bullying. And, by the way, it's not fun. Anyway, we wanted to help stop bullying because we felt bad about it because anything you say that sounds rude can count as bullying. And it's not cool and we knew that it's not funny. It's important to help people who are being bullied and stop the people who are bullying 'cause you don't want to stand in a situation like that. I just wanted to remind you about doing what's right.

Brown/Carter Family

The Candy Store

Debria Brown

· · · ❁ · · ·

IREMEMBER THAT WHEN I was young, my mother opened a candy and variety store. There was a small Jewish grocery store on the corner from our house about five doors down. And there was another smaller grocery store about four blocks from us in the opposite direction. We would have to cross the street to get to either one. The grocery that was farthest away was run by a very mean and cantankerous old man. It was located catty corner from our church. He hated children. He was belligerent and cruel and would yell at the children and snatch them by the arm. He was suspicious of everyone and once drew a gun on a group of school children to frighten them. My parents did not allow us to go alone to either store for a long time.

My mother decided to open a candy store to sell soda, cookies, chips, bread and milk to the neighbors to make it easy and safe for the children. There were five of us children in our family at the time. The little store became a success. After only a few months she was able to have the porch remodeled and signs posted. She obtained her retail license and displayed it proudly on the wall of the small store. She expanded the store inventory to include small toys, ice cream and household paper goods.

My older brother and I were so excited and proud of my mother and her little store. It was a family adventure. My father installed some new windows that could slide open to cool the store off on the hot summer days. My mother would allow us to be the merchants to the neighborhood children and would pay us with some small change and candy and treats. We weren't allowed to eat candy whenever we wanted but every now and then she would say "You all can help yourself to a penny's worth or a nickel's worth of candy." Sometimes she would pay us with the coins from the cigar box of cash. We all learned how to count money, make change, take inventory, balance the box, order stock, tell time and budget from the workings of the candy store.

Looking out the back door, I can see in my memory the long, clean sidewalk leading from the back gate to the door of the store where I was standing. She was able to install a fence and a new sidewalk in the back yard. Our back yard had a stand-alone pool, a swing set and sliding board for our enjoyment. When we weren't working, we would swim, play kick ball, dodge ball, jacks, marbles and jump rope in our safe, clean yard. When the other children would come to buy candy or goods, we would stop playing and go inside to make the sale of popsicles, chips or gum and many times the customers would stay and play in our yard with us for a while. I remember feeling happy, safe and blessed.

Debria Brown

Cake! Yum!

Debria Brown

· · · ❁ · · ·

My grandmother is going to bake a cake!
Her famous, delicious, yellow cake.
Made from scratch.
With homemade chocolate frosting…my favorite!
I can't wait…!!
And I get to help…this time.
No just sitting on the steps of the kitchen and watching—
Child under foot.
This time I can participate…
'Cause now…I'm eight!!

She brings out all the ingredients, before she starts,
serious and smiling the whole time.
Eggs, milk, butter, oil, water, cocoa, cream,
baking soda, baking powder, vanilla, flour and ice cubes.
Oh! And lots and lots of sugar.
She sets out the huge pink ceramic bowl, cool to the touch.
And now the monstrous noisy blender and all its parts.
First she measures the dry stuff and puts them in the bowl,
one after another. And now all the wet stuff, slowly, slowly.

The loud grinding turns all the single things
into a smooth, sweet, thick and creamy delight.

We are making progress!

She turns on the oven. "350 degrees," she says.
I peek in and the heat warms my face.
Now I can really help. I get to "grease and flour" the pans.
She lets me help to pour the mixture evenly into each pan
that will make the layer of the delicious mound.
I feel so important.

Now I get to lick the spatula
and drag my finger around the empty bowl
to get all the gooey batter!
She pretends not to see
as I put the bowl and utensils
into the hot soapy water of the sink to be washed.
I know my tummy will ache later.

When done I get a chance to eat my first piece of warm cake
made in the smaller pan made just for me.

The house is quiet and the aroma fills the house.
The anticipation is almost too much to bear.
After the cake cools
we get to put the creamy, thick chocolaty frosting on top of
and in between each fluffy layer.

After dinner I get to eat my second piece
with a tall glass of ice cold milk!
Yeah!

Debria Brown

Family Artifact

Debria Brown

· · · ❦ · · ·

ONE OF SEVERAL FAMILY ARTIFACTS that I treasure is a musical jewelry box that belonged to my grandmother. My mother's mother, Leota, owned a beautiful painted wooden jewelry box that, wonder of wonders, played music. I remember as a young girl seeing the jewelry box on her dressing table. As far as I could tell she rarely opened it. But when she would open it (mostly upon my insistent request), I would be transfixed by its seemingly magical beauty.

The box was painted black with a beautiful pink and green tropical scene over the dark background. Palm trees or weeping willows, something I had never seen before, billowed softly in the invisible breeze that made me think of far-away places. But the inside of the box was the most special. Once the beautiful box was opened, I could see the bright red velvet-like cloth interior and a small shiny mirror located just inside the lid. And once the lid was fully opened a tiny ballerina would spring up and start to twirl on her toes to the tinkling sounds of the song being played for her dance. I was thrilled.

I was the lucky and blessed granddaughter to inherit the prize. And to this day and on the rare occasion I open the jewelry music box, I am thrilled once again.

My Grandmother

Debria Brown

· · · ✿ · · ·

MY GRANDMOTHER WAS A PERSON of integrity and energy. My mother's mother had a hard life but she never complained or made excuses. She was always purposeful and intentional in her actions and speech. Upon meeting Leota you would learn right away that she was a no-nonsense personality. Her demeanor and speech would belie her size and beauty. She was a petite caramel-colored woman with lively dark eyes and strong hands. Lee, as my uncles and aunts called her, was a powerhouse. She was wise and made quick solid decisions. She moved quickly and everything in her path was made better and there was a reckoning in her quake.

All the children in her matriarchy affectionately called her "Gaw". It was a name my older brother called her first because he could not pronounce "grandmaw." The name stuck. Gaw was stern, hardworking and self-sacrificing. She loved my mother, Rosetta, the most and it was evident. My Mom was the youngest of her four children. Her love and care for my mother was how I learned to relax into her care and realize that underneath all the fussing and working and giving orders, she was a fiercely loyal and kind person. She loved differently from my mother. My mother was warm, funny, intelligent, patient, sweet and confident.

My grandmother always seemed to have some wise saying or advice on her lips, and a new technique or precise way of doing things to impart to anyone that was near. Especially the children. I remember her saying over and over again, "Make a place for things, and put things in their places". She maintained an immaculate house and was an excellent cook, although she barely ate anything. She baked the most delicious and beautiful lemon meringue pie, pecan pie, yellow cake with chocolate icing, fried chicken, baked yams and collard greens. She would make the most delicious iced tea and lemonade.

I now believe that because she was so focused, she seemed to be intimidating to some. Leota's mother died when she was a young mother herself and she had to raise four of her brothers and sisters along with her own growing family. She was family oriented and did not invest much in friends although she had many. I saw them as "hangers-on". Even late in her life I felt the extra people that came around to be in her presence were stealing time from me. She was not very physically demonstrative of her love, but she would warm up and cave in to our adoring hugs, kisses and shouts of glee when she would come to visit—although we knew it meant more work for us around the house, both before she arrived and for the duration of her stay. She was very proud of her grandchildren. She would brag to her neighbors about grades, talents and she ardently supported any school project or hobby.

I would love to hear my grandmother sing and hum. It was her entertainment along with watching the Lawrence Welk show. You had better be careful not to interrupt while that show was on television on Sunday nights. I learned several hymns by following her around and sitting outside her bedroom door. She would sing, "I come to the garden alone, while the dew is still on the roses, and the voice I hear falling on my ear was so sweet, the birds hush their singing…" She had her own version of singing the Christmas carol, "Silent Night." She would sing it like a marching song. I would get so frustrated and would say, "No, Gaw you have to string it out." She would smile and keep on singing. She also loved to sing the song, "Amen," sung by Sidney Poitier in the movie "Lilies of the Field." She would sing it with her own peppy beat rendition.

My grandmother was an early riser. She cleaned homes and ironed clothes for a living when her children were very young. Later she became employed at a local factory with several other family members and neighbors on the assembly line. She sent my mother to college on the money she earned. My grandmother divorced my grandfather after my mother was in high school. It was unusual for a woman to divorce in those days. I learned that she felt that it was too much of a burden for her to endure his long bouts of unemployment and unproductive ways. She could do bad all by herself. I felt embarrassed for some reason when I learned that they divorced. Yet, now I am divorced too. I didn't expect that to happen. She let my grandfather come to live in her house in his later years and when his health began to fail. I wouldn't do that. We called him Pawpaw. But she called him "David", "your grandfather," or "Mr. Osborne."

Leota always looked crisp and neat in her church usher uniform or her work uniform. Her thin curly hair was always in place. And when she put on lipstick she was perfectly adorned, ladylike and dressed up to me. Especially with her fox stole and fancy church hats.

My grandmother had asthma and suffered from the condition most of her adult life. It was diffi-cult for her to slow down. She eventually died from an enlarged heart after a long and satisfied life. I know her heart was too big for this world, and the Lord brought her home to be with Him.

Ode to Feelings of Loss and Sadness

Debria Brown

· · · ❀ · · ·

TIME FLIES.

Things change.

To me, I now realize that the evidence of things changing is proof that time has passed.

So quickly, noticeably and then again, not so much after all.

When I look back at the changes that have occurred, I realize I must also look for change in myself—the good, the bad, the focused and intentional and the inevitable yet not instantaneously aware.

As I drove around town after living away in California for many years, for some reason I felt disoriented and a little sad by the changes I saw in the once familiar landscape. There were new buildings that were once vacant spaces, and then there were vacant lots that once were the location of places I frequented in my life here. There were parks and most-needed green spaces, but more concrete and commercialism where once was community.

I met some of the people that had not moved on, although many had. Many of the ones left behind seemed isolated and sad, perhaps regretful, envious somehow. While others I encountered were joyous, resolved, successful and content that they had once lingered and floundered in life. Some people I had longed to see, others I was happy to avoid. My feelings changing indiscriminately on every occurrence.

My high school had closed down. Why had no one felt it important to share that information with me? The elementary school I attended had been torn down. The neighborhood streets seemed more narrow, the houses more dilapidated. The adults I knew were old, my colleagues seemed older which made me realize….so was I. But there were many new babies and taller children everywhere and throughout the family. What a joy!

New faces filled the positions of people I had cherished and honored such as my youth pastor, the neighborhood grocer. And places that I frequented or recognized, like the barbeque joint, the laundromat and the fish market were now closed or had moved to a new location. Neighbors and acquaintances had died or moved on.

But the sadness lifted and I am comforted in the realization that I had also changed and had moved on as well. And the fact is that I am better for it. My family and close friends are changing too, as are everyone and everything. Nothing remains the same and that can be good. The blessed assurance is that God never changes. My Lord, Jesus Christ is the same yesterday, today and forevermore. He knows me best and loves me still. I can rejoice in that!

Debria Brown

My Wild and Precious Life

Debria Brown

· · · ❁ · · ·

PRELUDE: THIS EVENING, BEFORE WRITING this piece, I received a message letting me know that a mutual friend had died. She was much younger than we both. This was the second person we had learned had died within this week.

I realize that my life is precious, if only because it is! And, I honor the giver of Life.

I admit that I don't always know what to do, nor do I profess to have a plan at all times for living it out. But I do know that I have been given a true gift, a chance to live. I must continue striving to give value, thanks and appreciation for that fact alone.

I am wild naturally, as we all are. The challenge is and the growth comes when we take the freedom we have to become tame enough to channel the energy constructively. To love, to give, to share, to create, to be the best we can from day to day, hour by hour until such time as it is all over… here.

Life is short, no matter how long we live. We have been given the freedom to grow into who we are and who we are going to be by striving, seeking, pondering, correcting and waiting on the ever-growing, changing and evolving you.

Who we are, is also an interaction with others. To make their lives enriched by your existence. And by taking others into your own. Many aspects of who we are, beyond how we look or sound are intangible. We are spirit, but we are affected and influenced by the lives of others, jointly. We must reach out for love and give it. Walk in peace to sustain it. Give to have. Seek to find. And ask to know.

Prayer, a conversation with God, our creator, can tell you who you are and who you were created to be. Express joy and focus on gratitude with thankfulness for this wild and precious life. Don't fear, for it is only False Evidence Appearing Real.

Music Sense Memory

Debria Brown

· · · ❁ · · ·

MUSIC IS IMPORTANT BECAUSE IT is and can be transformative. Music can make you face what it is you are feeling. It seems to heighten whatever emotion you are wont to express more deeply. The different genres can be selected to soothe, excite, encourage, distract, and speak to your soul, the seat of who you are.

I enjoy listening to a variety of music, such as gospel, jazz, blues, soul, symphony/orchestral, r & b, country and some rap. I can be transported to a different time and memory by the soulful renderings of some of my favorite artists' music.

As I have allowed myself to experience a variety of music, I have opened the expression, extension and enjoyment of the gift that music brings to my life, even though I am not particularly proficient in any musical instrumentation. I will sing, hum, dance, and shake to my favorite tunes with the abandon that is only relegated to the times I am engrossed in a song or tune. I am drawn in and discover that I am music and the rhythm is me.

In my early years, I remember thinking that people who talked back to the music were a little nuts. I decided that you could tell someone over the age of 25 by that very expression of joy. But now, let the right song hit me at the right time and I am the first one to break into the very saying I remember others saying and I shout, "Hey!" as I snap my fingers and sway. Or I will smile and close my eyes and shout, "That's it, that's my jam." That's so funny!

The Magical Bookstore: An Imaginary Place

Debria Brown

· · ·✤· · ·

THERE WAS A SMALL SHOP in the quiet part of the small town that was run by a sweet, mute woman and her cheerful and talkative husband. The shop was a bookstore. The name of the bookstore was Readers' World Book Shop. There weren't as many books on the shelves as some other bookstores and there were only 5 sections – fiction, non-fiction, religion, humor and poetry. There were no magazines, novelties, candy, gum or soda to be sold at the shop. Not even book marks, pens, reading glasses, t-shirts or key chains….just books! Rumor had it that the books just fly off the shelves and no one ever leaves without purchasing the very book they came in for.

Although the Shop was out of the way and off the beaten path, the shop was always busy. Busy, but not crowded. The bookshop never closed and every customer was completely satisfied with their purchase, even if they did not know what initially what they had come to purchase.

The shelves were made of wood and reached as high as the ceiling, creating unique rows and angles and cozy corners to hide, sit and read. Mr. and Mrs. O'Shea had owned the shop for the last 40 years. They were at the shop every day and oddly never looked tired, stressed or aged. No one had ever seen any deliveries being made to the shop, but there were always works by current authors, as well as at least one copy of every classic novel in every genre for purchase or perusal. Mr. O'Shea would share what he thought a customer might like to read or purchase, while Mrs. O'Shea only smiled and directed a customer to the right area of interest without a word and without the customer asking the first question of inquiry.

I had heard that there was some mystery about the process of the selection for purchase at this bookstore, so I decided I would check it out for myself. One Saturday morning I decided to drive to the little shop to observe the goings-on and perhaps to make a purchase. I drove and drove until reached the shop, which was not easy to find even though the directions were simple. The road that led to the gravel parking lot was unpaved. There were several large oak trees on the property and many blooming flowers and hanging baskets of plants and flowers on the gate, the fence and the porch.

The shop resembled a house more than a place of business. There had been no signs to direct someone to the locale; however, hanging on the gate and at the front entrance was a sign with the name of the shop and one that said "You Are Here."

As I entered the door, a small bell rang, but no one came to greet me. At the long front counter there was a welcome sign that read "Browse until your heart is content." I looked around and noticed several other customers seated and standing in different sections nearby reading and looking peaceful and intrigued.

I wandered to the poetry section and noticed that there were signed original copies of several of my favorite poets on the shelves! Nearby there was a big comfy chair under a large paned stained glass window. I sat down to begin to read. When I looked up Mrs. O'Shea was standing in front of me smiling and nodding...

Debria Brown

Joint Experience—Haibun (Meet the Artists)

Debria Brown

· · · ❁ · · ·

M Y SISTER, JANICE AND I went together to a function called "Meet the Artists" at the Central Library for an evening of fun and culture. It was an evening out for both of us. My sister is a busy hardworking business woman, wife and mother and this was a short, local outing for us. I am busy as well and I don't get to travel much these days, while she and her family are blessed to get away several times a year.

There was food, local authors, music, art, fashion, celebrities and magic. There was one world-famous local celebrity who came home to the city to speak at the event. We enjoyed meeting new people and talking with one another.

We had so much fun.
There was lots to do and see
For my sis and me.

There was a fashion show with beautiful, original and unique, colorful African fashion being modeled and sold. Musical performances were presented on stage while the audience was encouraged to sing along with the popular songs. A popular local gospel recording artist and his choir, an 80's band, dancers, soloists and poets graced the stage throughout the evening.

Gospel, jazz, and funk,
African fashion and style,
Spooky magic tricks.

Actress Vivica A. Fox gave an entertaining talk and a touching tribute to her mother. She gave a shout to this, her home town, and her classmates, relatives and friends as she regaled the audience with stories of her career and achievements. One other of the acts that stood out to me was a so-called magic act. The magician called himself an illusionist, but most of his performance or act was so shocking that they were beyond the everyday sleight of hand. The majority of his act was truly from the dark side or the occult.

A home grown beauty
Vivica Fox is her name.
Acting is her game.

Over all it was a fun night to remember. Shared with my friend, my sister.

Where I'm From

Debria Brown

$\cdots \maltese \cdots$

I am from strong love…
committed, kind and proud.
Her eyes, his thighs,
I am a quiet storm.

I am from hot sun, warm smells, good food, contentment and endurance.
Simple games, teamwork…kickball, dodge ball, hopscotch and bikes…
bubblegum, popsicles, 45's, LPs' and jazz.
Soul music, gospel and a little bit o' country.

I am from packing us all up and going to the park,
the drive-in and picnics until after dark.

Waiting for Daddy to come home to feel safe and protected.
His first born girl of six with my sisters following,
and with four more that are boys, my brothers.
Home with Mama before and after school,
long conversations about whatever with ease and confidence,
trying new things with their encouragement.
I am from faithfulness, and support in all I endeavor.
Trying my wings to do whatever.

I am from sing, laugh, play, and dream.
He drank his coffee black. She drank hers with cream.

I am from learning how to trust myself
and to tolerate others.
Knowing who I am
and respecting my dad and my brothers.

I am a helper, a believer, a queen.
Taught to love God and to see Him in everything.
I am from looking for the best in everyone…
trying hard to be serious, when life is plain fun!

Debria Brown

List Poem

Debria Brown

· · ·⚘· · ·

A cool breeze blows the leaves of the fully-grown tree
as the bird sits and sings about the beauty of the scene.
The warm yellow sun kisses the bright green leaves
as the caterpillar crawls underneath as it seeks the meal
of the red lady bug inching along.
Colorful balloons float by against the blue sky
that have escaped the hands of the children playing nearby.
The sound of their laughter startles the bunnies and squirrels
and they scamper away towards the brook nearby.
The graceful swan floats on the serene pond which reflects on the window
from which I see all the activity
from my wheelchair in my room.

Acronym Poem

Debria Brown

...⊛...

Father, foundation, fearless, faithful, fun, free
All together, amazing
Memorable, mobile, miraculous, motion, milestones, mother
Intense, intelligent, insistent
Legitimate, lovely, laughter, lively, loving
Year-round celebration, yelling, yearning to belong

My Old Neighborhood

Debria Brown

· · · ❀ · · ·

I SUPPOSE A NEIGHBORHOOD IS made up of more than just the houses, buildings and streets. A neighborhood is made up of the people who live and work within those parameters, too. And the events, sights and sounds that reside and accompany their lives.

I have only lived in my current neighborhood for a few short years and it is very different from the two or three communities that I grew up in as a child and young adult. I believe that it takes time to form a neighborhood. So I will describe the one that I spent most of my young life.

As a young girl, I grew up in a cohesive neighborhood with my family. I attended all of my elementary school career at the same school. The school was in walking distance. We lived in a small three-bedroom house with a large fenced backyard. In the one block area of the two streets adjoined by an alleyway, there were at least 105 school-age children that I can count and remember. Most of us all went to the same school because all but about six were high school age. When I lived in this neighborhood our family was small, Mama, Daddy, two brothers, four sisters and me. We didn't really feel that we were bustin' at the seams until Mama was about to have our last little sister. There was hardly any room for our two older step-brothers, who would come for the summers.

We lived next door to a family of grown men and their elderly parents and one aunt. All of them were raging alcoholics, except the father. Most every weekend they would present a drunken brawl and the police would be called out, while the whole neighborhood would come out for the show. On the other side of our house was our neighbor Mrs. Burris. She lived in a huge two-story home with a basement/cellar. Her yard was immaculate with a beautiful flower garden. She was old and always angry. She hated children, but tolerated my sisters and brothers and me. For some reason, she doted on me.

On one corner, about four houses down, was a small Jewish grocery store. The butcher there was a friend of my father's. The grocery had small aisles where barely two carts could pass going in the opposite direction at once. The grocer sold canned goods, bread, bar soap, detergent, soda, a few hair products, a few wilted vegetables, hosiery and candy. Which as you can imagine was quite popular with the children of the neighborhood.

Across from the grocery was a barber/beauty shop and a store front church. At the other end of the block was a popular barbeque joint, another church and a used clothing store. The local library branch, which was one of my favorite haunts, was a mere four blocks away. Most of the children had bicycles, homemade skate boards or go-carts, roller skates, and some type of ball. We played for hours in the alley, under the hot sun. Kickball, dodge ball, tag, marbles, cowboys and Indians, dress-up, dolls, races, basketball, jacks, school and jump rope. In the evening we would play hop-scotch, sight games, and have great arguments, debates and conversations, including tall tales, flat out fabrications, and stories of the spooky sort. Alliances were formed, battle lines drawn, scrapes and fights won and lost. Revenge and forgiveness were learned. Lifetime friendships were forged.

It was safe to play outside for the children. All the parents knew one another and most families were from two-parent homes. The men worked hard and most of the mothers were stay-at-home wives. Most of the adults, as well as the children and the merchants, knew one another by name and family. We all celebrated the holidays as a community, even though there were at least three different religious denominations or faiths, and everyone helped everyone else out as they could.

Neighborhoods can become part of the fabric of one's life. I hope to always be on a good patch wherever I reside.

Debria Brown

My Neighborhood Now

Debria Brown

· · · ✿ · · ·

I HAVE NOT LIVED IN my neighborhood for too long, about five years. I am buying my home there. I am feeling my way and beginning to relax and feel safe, secure and comfortable there. My house is the first house on the corner, next to a huge vacant grassy lot. Across from my property is another large house and next to it is an urban apartment complex of about six units. I have only seen someone at the house twice in the years I have lived there. The resident families in the apartment complex come and go about every twelve months or so. Next to the house across the street is another huge vacant grassy lot where another home once stood.

I live next door to my neighbors who purchased their home and moved in almost exactly one year before me. They are a married couple who are friendly and basically quiet. They have been married for over 25 years. Recently the wife's mother has moved in with them. The wife talks really loudly and takes a long time to say what it is she is talking about. She is very detailed in every conversation. Her husband is quiet and has few words. Which is fine with me. The wife talks enough for all of us and we all just, smile, nod and respond with as few words as are left to say.

My neighbor knows everything that goes on in our block and perhaps the next 2-3 blocks away. She talks to everyone. She keeps me informed. We look out for one another's property and stay alert for any emergency. The neighbor on the other side of the couple is another single lady. She is a property owner and has purchased at least two other properties in the area. She is friendly and is near retirement age as well. She renovated the house where she lives and does most of the work with her own hands.

On most holidays, when there are fireworks, I can sit on my massive front porch and watch the colorful, explosive shows from near and far without leaving the comfort of home. The vacant lot next to my home is owned by a local church and the property behind mine is owned by another local Christian fellowship. On warm days, some of the fellowship and/or the church come out on their property to pray and sing praises to God. They witness to passersby about the goodness of God and tell of the way to salvation and eternal life in heaven. They play uplifting music and I feel encouraged and comforted.

Across the street is a long standing fish market and candy store. It has been in the neighborhood for decades, or so I have been told. I have not visited the premises as yet. On occasion, I hear the blaring sound of a fire truck or emergency van rushing by, on an urgent mission from the firehouse three streets away. Our street is one of the two main thoroughfares in the area on which the emergency vehicles can safely pass at the high rate of speed. The traffic on my street is just as steady at night as it is during the day.

I have trees that line the southern side of my property, as well as across the street from my house. I love to watch the changing seasons in their leaves, branches and blossoms. On occasion, when I have the time and energy, I take a walk around the neighborhood. I have one sister that has built her home two streets over to the east of mine. We have another sister that built her home one street west of mine. My church is less than one-half mile away, and I work less than 20 minutes from home.

I have a bicycle and, in the past summers, I have taken a ride to the nearby library and to the local donut shop and bakery. Most of the people I encounter in my neighborhood are civil and we all smile and wave or nod to one another. I believe if we had a common cause, at least in our block, we would be cohesive and civil. I have become comfortable and familiar in the atmosphere of my neighborhood and I have so much for which to be grateful.

When I Feel Most at Home

Debria Brown

· · · ❀ · · ·

I FEEL MOST AT HOME when I am at home. I also feel at home when I am at one of my sister's houses. The feeling is one of comfort, relaxation, freedom and acceptance and love. At my home it is peaceful. When I am at home and I have time to be there without having to rush around or leave to go, time is not a hindrance and is only relevant to my intention and mood.

I am content at home when I have good food, snacks, and supplies stored away. When I have cleaned the house and everything is neat, clean and fragrant and the temperature is just right. I don't mind the clutter of my books, magazines and writing materials. I love pillows and throws for comfort. I will wear whatever crazy, comfy, loose garments, wraps and socks that suit my fancy at the time, or my fluffy house slippers. I don't like to go barefoot.

At home, I can choose to watch a good movie, listen to jazz or gospel or read one of my many books on my four book cases. Sometimes I choose to journal, or study the Bible or I prepare for a class I am taking or teaching. Sometimes I just want to pray and sing praises to the Lord.

Sometimes, I take the time to paint my nails, give myself a facial and pedicure or take a long warm, sudsy bath. I fiddle around in my clothes closets or sit on my deck and watch the sunset. I am still getting acclimated to my kitchen in this house, but sometimes I will try new recipes in my spare time.

When I watch television, my favorite genre is cooking shows, decorating and home improvement. I live alone, so most times it is quiet. Unless I am having a phone conversation with a friend, family member or mentee. And sometimes when I am alone and I am watching the news, or the preposterous talk shows, reality TV, judge shows and game shows, I will talk back to the television and give my considered opinion about the goings-on. This has been a recent development in my routine as I grow older. As it also seems the volume has to be increased to provoke my involvement.

When I am comfortable at home I will daydream about life scenarios and places I would like to visit. I am a kind hostess in my home and I have the gift of hospitality but overall, I prefer to be entertained casually with intimate repartee in the comfort of friends.

I enjoy clean comedy and I love to laugh. I don't know if my sense of humor is much shared by many others, except for my best friend and a couple of my sisters. So, I remain secretly amused and enjoy my own candor and creative humorous thoughts. I smile a lot.

I am not beautiful to everyone, but I am comfortable in my own skin. I love others and I feel most at home wherever I feel loved and accepted.

Watching My Sister, Janice, Tell Her Favorite Birthday Story

Debria Brown

· · · ✤ · · ·

I AM WATCHING AND LISTENING to my sister tell me about one of her favorite birthday memories. My sister begins to share with me the excitement and privilege she felt when three of our other sisters gave her a sleepover birthday party.

She turned to me and said, "Ooh, let me tell you about my birthday party that Rita and the twins gave me when I turned 13." Her beautiful dark eyes sparkled as she leaned forward and spoke breathlessly.

"Okay", I said. I faintly recall the fact that she did have a party that year. I would not have been present and able to participate. There are 11 years difference in our ages and 5 siblings between us. I was already living away from home. Three of the four sisters her senior were generous enough to give her an indulgent sleepover.

"So, I had a slumber party when I turned 13. It was great! They let me invite all my friends over for the party and the sleep over at the house." She counted on her fingers as she named some of her running buddies. One by one she named at least eight little girls that had been allowed to come to her party and stay the night at our family home. I do remember having met some of her friends over the years. They all had attended the same elementary school together and had grown to that age right in the neighborhood. And now they were embarking on their high school days together. Her cheeks were flushed with excitement as she named the food that was served and the games they played.

"They had everything there good to eat…popcorn, pizza, chips, soda, and cake? We stayed up Alllll night!! We danced, sang to our favorite music, played games and we told jokes. I think we even tried to have a pillow fight. I think we all must have slept downstairs in the living room and dining room on the sofas and the floor in sleeping bags." She laughed. I laughed too. "Uh huh, it was so fun! I got several really nice gifts, from everybody." She nodded her head and smiled. "The next day, my sisters cleaned up and took some of my friends home. They all said they had a great time. I know I did." She practically squealed, as she stared off in space. "It is a good memory."

When I relayed my observation of her telling her story, I mentioned how it was really so nice of our sisters to give her a party with all the "fixins" considering how mischievous she was as a child. She terrorized her older sisters and was a little brat. She would chase them around, with them screaming, with a dead mouse or a bug. She would play pranks on them and then laugh and run really fast so they couldn't catch her. She was always feisty and fun. She would not back down from a fight either. She would take down anyone that would come for her, boy or girl, bully or not. She was quick with her tongue and thought most things were funny, even if they weren't. She would get a kick out of aggravating our youngest sister until the baby would pin her down and attempt to bite her face off. Then she would scream for deliverance while laughing the whole time.

She would not admit to tormenting our siblings. I have always known her to be a spitfire, and I think she is funny. I remember when I would call home to talk with our mother and she would share all of the antics of my siblings at home. This sister would be the one about which there were the most prolific stories. Mainly about how she or Daddy would have to "go up to the school," because my sister had gotten into "another fight". She was little (short for her age), but a mighty mite. I love my little sister and would not change her or trade her in for anyone. She is family and she is my friend.

Debria Brown

My Sister, Debria, Telling the Story of Her Favorite Birthday

Janice Carter

· · · ✿ · · ·

MY MOST MEMORABLE BIRTHDAY WAS the year I had two surprise birthday parties given for me. One day on a significant birthday, almost fourteen years ago now, I was given a surprise birthday party by my siblings. This first party was on the actual day. The second surprise party was given the next day by my husband. I really enjoyed them both and, yes, they were a huge surprise! I couldn't stop smiling because not only was I surprised, but I was shocked and embarrassed that they were able to pull it off without my knowing about it in advance...a true surprise. I know, know. People always say they were surprised by a party, but I would always be suspicious that they had been able to detect the covert goings on prior to the event. However, me being the oldest, (or shall I say, first) daughter of the family of eleven, I thought I could not ever be surprised by them planning a party for me, if they ever would. I just never suspected or expected the honor. You see, I just knew that I could detect any sneaky or suspicious behavior they would be up to because I thought I kept my finger on the pulse of what was happening in my family.

My family is very close. I talk to most of my sisters almost daily. I talk with my brothers quite often, as well. We share a lot of what is going on in our lives regularly. We had just lost our dear mother to cancer not too many years prior, and through her illness, care and demise we seemed to have drawn even closer, as some of them were just starting out with their own families. We still celebrate her life on her birthday and we call it Angel Day.

Since my mother's passing, I am usually the one that initiates and plans our family outings. This is how it went down. My birthday, July 22, was on a Thursday that year. I had heard from everyone by the late afternoon. It is our family tradition to call one another on our birthdays and to begin the day with pleasant greetings and blessings. Often, if there was to have been a get-together, the honoree would have already planned something or invited everyone to stop by if they wanted to. I had not planned anything that year at all. I was going to go home and rest to celebrate a quiet evening with my husband. I was content and happy, and had planned to take off the following day to do a little pampering and, perhaps, a little shopping.

I called my sister upon leaving work to see how she was doing and she told me that she had been napping. She asked me to stop by her house on the way home, if I would. I figured she may have a little gift for me or just wanted a hug.

Upon arrival, I saw one of my older brothers approaching her house, as well. He rarely comes out for visiting, but I thought nothing of it. I was happy to see him. We hugged. He wished me a happy birthday again, as he had called me earlier. As we approached the door, he stepped back and my sister snatched open the door with a big smile and everyone was behind her, yelling, "Surprise," and singing the "Happy Birthday" song. Cameras were flashing and I got plenty of food, money, hugs, and gifts.

Everyone knew that I was truly surprised and they enjoyed the party all the more. More friends, more of the family and fun and food and flowers, and photos and music and fun and love. Ha! They got me good! I loved it. I will be on the lookout for the next big surprise!

Janice Carter

The Barbecue

Janice Carter

· · · ⟨❁⟩ · · ·

THIS IS PRETTY MEMORABLE TO me. The dates may be a little forgotten, but around January, 1999, I was invited to a barbeque over to a good friend of mine's house. She wanted me to meet a friend of her boyfriend's. We met and had fun. I remember talking to the guy on the phone a couple of times after we met. The next week, I got another invite to her house for another BBQ date with her, her boyfriend, and his best friend for me.

When I got there, my friend, her boyfriend, and his brother were there. I was introduced to the brother. He approached me with a very smooth greeting, along with a kiss to the hand. I blushed and asked where my supposed date was. They laughed and said he was on his way. But, let me back up. I actually think I was impressed with the brother. He was very handsome, dressed nice, and smelled very good. I was looking very nice myself, I might add.

Once the date arrived, we ate dinner and laughed and talked. Across the room, I kept noticing the brother watching me and winking and blowing kisses at me, trying to get my attention. At the end of the date, when I was about to leave, the other gentleman wanted to walk me out to my car, but the brother walked me out instead. The Brother called me the next day, which was Super Bowl Sunday. He was so mild-mannered, funny, nice, and charming. He told me he fell in love with me at first sight. We got married one year later. Now, nineteen years later, we are still together. We have been through lots with health concerns, but he is still the same.

My Journey to California

Janice Carter

· · ·✿· · ·

AROUND THE SUMMER OF '87, I decided to move to Cali to be with my family. I was leaving my husband and took our two children. I didn't have much money, so we traveled by bus. That's a story never to be replayed. It took three-and-a-half days to get there. Many stops, lots of stress, crying, anxiety and loneliness.

At the Daycare

Wake up, get dressed,
Rush out the door,
Thinking of what lies ahead for my day.
The talking, singing, walking dancing.

I Remember

I remember last night I couldn't sleep, but I was so tired.
I remember once I left the house I forgot to take my medicine
I remember I needed to buy milk after I left the grocery store.
I remember that I can do all things through Christ, who strengthens me.
I remember why I can't write stories—'cause I can think them up in my head but can't put them on paper without forgetting.

List Poem

Janice Carter

· · · ❀ · · ·

I wake up on Saturday to the bright sunlight,
I think of what to do,
I try to make my list right.
I start off with a prayer, this is not rare.
I give my legs a try by hitting the floor,
knowing I won't get back in the bed anymore.
I'm thinking what to do first,
Get showered, dressed, eat and clean,
Then the phone rings…and I have to change my plans.
The caller says there's a sale…
I can't resist, I shop 'til I drop.
Then the alarm goes off at 5:00 am.
Today is Monday!

Memories of the Corner
at 17th & Delaware Street

Janice Carter

· · · ✾ · · ·

I REALLY THINK OF A few memories from this corner from years ago. I was married to my first husband and we lived on the northeast corner in an apartment building. I was young, with one infant daughter. The apartment was very small, like an attic that I could only enter and exit through the back. At night, I was so scared. Especially when my husband wasn't there with me and the baby. I remember the first Sunday morning my parents came to pick me and my baby up for church and I told my mother how scared I was. I really don't remember how long after that that we stayed in that dump, but it wasn't long before I was rescued by my parents. I can't really remember where we moved from there at this point. But I'm sure my dad, a pastor, wouldn't have had us move into the family house.

My next memory from this corner is the church that is next to this building. It had a daycare in the basement. It was probably three to four years later from living in the dumpy apartment across the street. I worked at the White Castle restaurant on 16th and Illinois Street. I took my daughter to the daycare and walked to work. My daughter was very outgoing. I remember once she fell off the jungle gym and bumped her head. She had a really big cartoon knot on her head that left a bruise. I was very mad at the time. But kids will have falls. I remember the building across the street. My new memory of this corner is going to be me and my sister participating in the WORD DANCE program.

My World

Janice Carter

· · · ❁ · · ·

THE SPACE OF MY UNIVERSE is not that big. It is filled with very important planets that are necessary to survive.

Space is so occupied that there isn't any room for intruders.

There are two slits for one to see out of, like a window. There is a round object with two holes where air and smells come in the small space…some good, some bad.

There is a large opening that takes in plenty of goods and lets out plenty of sounds, there are two parts on either side, only one works actively. The other is broken and is just there for looks.

In the center of this universe is a small planet about the size of a pea, which is the major function of the whole universe.

Sometimes it gets cloudy and foggy, sometimes it runs like a charm. Without this universe full of planets I would be nothing.

Over all it's very loving, caring and faithful.

As the planets operate in the universe collectively, it moves from place to place, working very hard to nurture others, aliens to show people the goodness in themselves. Helping them with their future goals.

As the planets operate together, it works hard with lots of operational tasks from start to finish.

Wild and Precious Life

Tim Carter

. . . ✿ . . .

WHAT I PLANNED TO DO with my wild and precious life was to go to college and get a good job, but that didn't work out. I had three goals. I had to take care of being wild, not listening to my mother, doing worldly things. I got caught up in the world and finally things started getting real. Your kids, your parents, your wife, your health, your church, and God. I went through a dramatic surgery later in my life and it made me know how precious this life is—so precious to me now. I don't take anything for granted in this life I have. The world didn't give it and can't take it away.

The Dixons

Hank

Keesha Dixon

· · · ✿ · · ·

I REMEMBER MY COUSIN HANK. Now that is the most strangest of all memories to recall on April 17, 2018 after participating in an "I Remember" writing exercise. Why? Because Hank wasn't my cousin, although most people thought he was because we were just two years apart. He was my nephew. He was younger and smaller in frame than I was. He was very dark skinned because he was a "blue baby" when he was born. He had the most beautiful round eyes. They were dark, too, but the whites of his eyes were a pearly white. His lips and his gums were dark which made his teeth very white. And his skin was oh so smooth.

I remember that when all of the "cousins" were at play, Hank would fatigue much too soon. He would have to rest to catch his breath. The elders told us that was because he was a "blue baby" when he was born.

I never truly understood that blue baby reference except there was something wrong with his heart. It had a hole in it. Yes, Hank couldn't play for long periods because he would get winded, but he would try until he got tired.

As we got older, he became sicklier. There were more doctor's visits and then those turned into hospital stays. I remember one day hearing that Hank was going into the hospital and he would be there for a while because they were going to fix the hole he had in his heart. He was 10 years old and I was 12.

Mother told me I would not be able to visit him while he was in the hospital. None of the kids could.

It was raining that day. It was a very gloomy day as I looked out of the kitchen window. There wasn't a lot of traffic flowing on either side of Loomis which was a two-way street. The rain came down like someone was pouring it from a bucket. Then I saw my Mom's car pull off the street and into the garage.

Through the rain she walked and came in the door, walking up those three steps into the kitchen and never really looking at me. As she passed, on her way to her room, she said quickly, "Hank is gone."

That was it, "Hank is gone." And then she vanished, shutting the door to her room, where she stayed for I can't remember how long. My gaze returned to the window, looking at the rain as it fell hard against the ground. I stood there not knowing what to feel, how to feel, what to say and who to say it to.

I remember my nephew, Mack Hank Connor. He'd been named after his father. He was my sister's first child. She was sixteen when she had him. I remember the last picture that was taken of him when he was alive. It sat on the table between two chairs for many years. He had on white pajamas that had blue markings on them. He was smiling as he stood beside his hospital bed.

He was alive in that picture and now he was lying in a casket with my sister crying hysterically over his body. I saw him from a distance because I couldn't bear to look at him up close. He was dressed in a black suit with a white shirt and black tie.

I guess I will always remember my nephew, Hank. He was the first close relative that died when I was but a child.

July 5, 2005

Keesha Dixon

···❁···

July 5, 2005 was the day I gave my key to my Mother's house back to her
in the presence of Lola, my elder sister.

It was the day after Lola's 65th birthday celebration.
It was the day after my Mother had looked at me in such an accusatory way.
It was the day after my mother verbally intended to hurt my feelings.
It was the same day Lola told me she believed Mother was suffering from dementia.
It was the same day my sister told me Josie, my cousin, was going through the same thing with her
Mom, my Aunt Mattie.

July 5, 2005 was the day I gave my key to my Mother's house back to her
in the presence of Lola, my only sister.

It was the same day my Mother let me know she still thought I had a key to her bedroom.
It was the same day my Mother said she still believes my husband had keys to her house.
It was the same day my Mother stated things keep coming up missing from her house because we,
my husband and I, still had those keys. She was sure we'd had duplicates made.

July 5, 2005 was the day I gave my key to my Mother's house back to her
in the presence of Lola, my only sister.

It was the same day I cried as I drove away from my Mother's house.
It was the same day my heart broke so deeply.

It was the same day I came to realize my Mother was truly delusional and suffering.

It was the same day I went home feeling lost, bewildered and unsure.

It was the same day I prayed to God for His help. "I need you now, Lord".

It was the same day I realized how much more praying I would need to do

if I wanted to keep my sanity as I watched my Mother age

knowing in my spirit I, too, would travel this road.

It was the same day I tried to recall Ephesians Chapter 6 Verse 12

 and the only words I could remember was we wrestle not with flesh.

It was the same day I realized this was yet another ploy of the devil to shake my faith.

It was the same day I looked up, not down and recognized there is still hope.

It was the same day I wrote these words so I would not forget the evolution of my Mother's life.

July 5, 2005 was the day I gave my key to my Mother's house back to her
in the presence of Lola, my elder sister. A date to remember.

I Need to Be Me

Keesha Dixon

· · · ❁ · · ·

This is all I ask…Give me the freedom
        to explore my "mee-dom."
Can't you just let me be?
        I am who God made me to be.
I am not you—I am me.
        Kinky hair, round eyes, dark skin…naw we ain't kin.
I am my name
        stop the game
            we are not the same.
I am me and you are you, can't I do I and still be true?
        I refuse to be less
Just cause you think you are more
        that alone don't make you su-pe-ri-or.
I am passing through, living God's plan for as long as I can.
        So I know I won't be here long making sense of right and wrong.
Time will fade be not afraid, save your jade and just let me
        Be

The Walker

Keesha Dixon

· · · ❀ · · ·

I'VE BEEN LIVING ON THIS corner for over thirty-three years. It is a very busy intersection with lots of bus, car and pedestrian traffic. Being a people watcher, I enjoy the diversity I get to see every day.

I've watched her for about two years now. She replaced another young lady who grew haggard quickly and then disappeared. Wow, she got new hair this year. A brilliant red bob-cut wig. You know the shade, almost iridescent. She's thin in frame, somewhat shapely, about 5'7" with a small pot belly. No, she's not pregnant. Her complexion is caramel-colored but there is an odd ash to it. She has round eyes and a smile that only appears when she is trying to flag down someone, which doesn't happen often but when it does, she is intentional. I'd guess her age to be late twenties, but she looks older in the face.

Every now and then she'll yell at a passing vehicle or wave at someone a few blocks down. But for the most part she walks and walks and walks day in day out until late at night, but not all night. Although there is an occasional nod of the head, she rarely makes eye contact especially when she's carrying on a conversation on her cell phone. She's very animated when she's talking, hand waving and strutting with a long gait.

One morning, I was working in my garden. She was walking by. I looked up and our eyes met briefly. I said, "Good morning." She replied, "Good morning" without breaking stride. I said, "You be careful out here today." She said, "I will" still walking. My glaze followed her until she went down the alley once again.

Shoveling Snow

Robert Steven Dixon

· · ·✥· · ·

EARLY ONE SATURDAY MORNING AS I woke up I realized it had snowed. Jumping out of bed, I decided today I can make a few dollars shoveling snow for some neighbors. My brother had the same idea, but we had different neighbors to contend with. He went his way and I went mine.

The names escape me now, but as I made my way in the snow I stopped by Mr. & Mrs. so and so, the first neighbor's house who lived nearby. "Can I shovel your walk, Sir?" The answer was either yes or no as I went along. At each house, the same question and answer. After several houses I had made a few dollars (don't remember how much). Then, it dawned on me "It's cold out here." Having not checked the weather before I left it must have been below zero. Here I was several blocks from home. I said to myself, "Self, you better get home and get warm."

The picture in my mind was the pot belly stove in the middle of the room. That thought was my only saving grace trudging back to the house. The closer I got to the house, the colder I got. By the time I got in the door, my fingers were all but froze and my feet were as cold as ice. Once I got inside the door, I stood by the potbelly stove for at least half an hour to get warm.

To My Mother, Martha Dixon: Lesson Learned

Robert Steven Dixon

· · ·✿· · ·

MY MOTHER WAS A SMOKER. In fact everyone around her smoked. You'd see it on TV advertisements with the Marlboro Man as he took a long drag on his cigarette. I thought that was cool. All my aunts smoked, too. One in particular was Aunt Novella. Although now, I don't think she really was my aunt. Back then everyone was called aunt or uncle or cousin to show some family ties.

Aunt Novella was a little different, she never really smoked cigarettes. They were more like a prop. Aunt Novella was always dressed. She wore dresses with high heeled shoes and above the knee nylon stockings. I knew this because she always found some excuse to tighten or straighten or pull on them. She took great glee in showing her ankles and, as a ten year old boy, I found it very intriguing. I could never go to Aunt Novella's house by myself.

Anyway my mother was a smoker, just like on the TV advertisements with the Marlboro Man, who took a long drag on his cigarette. She would hold the cigarette, always upright, between two fingers on the left. The ash would linger on top 'til it got about an inch long before she would flick it into the ashtray. I thought that was so cool. One day, I asked could I smoke. She said that I was too young. So I waited.

Round about sixteen years old, my friends and I were in a 1965 Ford Mustang. There were six of us. Someone pulled out a cigarette. We all decided to smoke it. After having passed around the cigarette to everyone else, it was finally my turn. I decided to do as my Mother did, as seen on TV advertisements with the Marlboro Man. I inhaled long. Suddenly, my face got hot, my eyes watered up, my lungs closed off. I started choking, I started flailing around, yelling, "I can't breathe, I can't breathe!" My friends panicked and rushed me to the hospital.

They called my mother. She came in, looked at me and said, "Told you, you were too young to smoke."

My mother was a smoker…I am not.

Jones/Lisenby Family

I Remember My Aunt

Brittany Jones

· · · ❁ · · ·

I remember seeing her smile.

I remember hearing her laugh.

I remember her heels.

I remember her wine glasses.

I remember our last conversation.

That laugh, that's the thing I remember the most about her.
It was infectious.
"Hey Punkin!" she said.
I was so glad to hear her voice. "How are my babies?" She loved Kylah and Kamrynn.
She would take Kylah into her room and close the door. Then dare us to bother them.
She would let them play dress up in her heels and makeup.
Just like she did with me.
See, I was the only girl. Her three sons and me. So I think we both needed the girl time.
My mom could have killed her for buying me my first makeup set at nine years old.
I've loved a "Beat face" since then.
She was there when I had my girls and spoiled them like she did me.
The day she left I somehow knew I would never see her again.

I was crushed, she was my favorite person on the planet
and I made sure she knew it every time I talked to her.
I cried like a baby, though no one knew it.
I was thrilled to tell her about niece number three.
She would have loved her to pieces. Only that conversation was our last.
She was one of the most resilient people I knew, she never let her
trials, her pain, her flaws or shortcomings define her.
She taught me one of the most important lessons of my life,
never forget to laugh,
always bring your heels and have fun.

Brittany Jones

Gumbo Day

Brittany Jones

· · · ❀ · · ·

Crawfish, shrimp; collard greens
And all other manner of delicious-ness.
It's Gumbo Day and nobody makes gumbo like my Daddy.
It only took us months to convince him to make it.
Gumbo, crab cakes, and fried alligator. The perfect combo.
Creole goodness but we're not from the Nola.
We call ourselves the two-plate family.
My stepmom's peach cobbler makes it all complete!
Gumbo Day means quality time with sisters, which makes it all complete.
Girl talk, niece loving, dance battles, makeup tips, beauty trends, Facebook gossip.
Operation Gumbo Day Success

Music

Brittany Jones

· · ·✿· · ·

Music, it's ingrained in my spirit
Music runs through my veins
Music, I breathe it
Stephanie Mills, Al Jarreau, Earth, Wind, and Fire, Herbie Hancock
Lutha, Michael, and Johnny Gill
are the soundtracks to my childhood.
Learning every line to "The Wiz," every song in "Dream Girls,"
every dance move in the Jackson 5 movie.
Nas, Tupac, Biggie, Wu-Tang,
Bone-Bone-Bone-Bone...it's the 1st of the MONTH WAKE UP!
I'm A Survivor, that likes a Soldier, that I was So Weak in the Knees
I asked myself Who Can I run To?
We were just Kickin' It
So I decided to keep it, My Little Secret.
Before I knew it I was Dangerously In Love.
Music, it's the fabric that sews my family together.
My great-grandfather's guitar
My grandfather's guitar
Orlando, my daddy's guitar
Kylah's guitar
Kylah's voice, smooth like velvet and brings tears to my eyes.
Kamrynn feeling the rhythms in her feet.

Majorette, Jazz, Ballet.
Kynzi's little voice belting out ABCD
O-O-O at the top of her lungs.
Drums with Laurea.
Dance parties with Jamia.
Clara singing opera in notes that reach heaven.
Lauren and Khadijah and me as the 3 Heartbeats, and never missed a step

List Poem—Music

Kylah Jones

· · · ✾ · · ·

The vibrant sounds of
Music fill my head
Every time I lay down in my bed I feel the love
In my heart, the sounds of the beat,
par-rum-papa-pum, the sound of
guitar strings, hitting my thumbs,
the sounds of harmonizing
with my Mom, singing Alicia Keys at midnight,
But sometimes I have a judgement of me.
Having a hard time is it wrong or
is it right? Do I sing like this or
that? When I'm laying down in
bed contemplating what's in my head
I think of my Pawpaw.

Music, Oh Music

Kylah Jones

. . . ✿ . . .

Music, oh, Music
The pain, sorrow, sadness
And even happiness
The endless stories they can tell
When you sick and not doing well
They can be the remedy that can be
Used on any device, any app, ranging
From IPod, to Samsung, and Apple music, to Sound Cloud
They can be put on a playlist
Ready screaming for you to hit play
and sing along
losses, breakups, depression
things that are controversial in our world today anyone can
put either bias into or even the truth
especially the truth that hurts can be easily understood in a song
Music, Oh Music

Paw Paw

Kylah Jones

· · · ✿ · · ·

Car rides with my Paw Paw
Days I remember with my Paw Paw Byrd
Going over to my grandma's house but really going to my PawPaw.
He would give me a great big hug, take me to the park with my cousins, Jayda,
Kennedy, and Stephan. We would go on car rides and play
"Who knows the song better?"
and he would say "Girl what you know about this?"
then when I beat him he would say "Girl how you know all these songs."
Even though he's gone he still lives in my heart
along with the great times and memories he gave me.
My Paw Paw told me a story before he died and said that when I was a baby
I screamed a lot and he said, "That baby can sing."

Along Came Baby

Kamrynn Lisenby

· · · ❀ · · ·

I woke up 12.7.2016 to my mother groaning.
She called my grandmother and announced, "I don't feel good."
I remember it was my birthday. I sang "Happy Birthday" to me.
I got dressed and woke up my sister.
I went into the kitchen and made myself a bowl of cereal.
I turned on the TV and watched my favorite show Teen Titans Go.
My grandmother came to my house and picked all three of us.
We rode the bus to school.
Mom called my Great Grandmother's house and said she is having the baby today.
At least that's what she told me after school.
My presents were in the corner
and we grabbed them and put them in the trunk.
December 7, 2016 was the day Kynzi was born.
Why did she have to come on my birthday?
Mommy said, "Just enjoy your cake and presents."
Kynzi is now 16 months old and bossy.
She runs the whole house.

Macaroni

Kamrynn Lisenby

· · ·❁· · ·

I ate macaroni
That's my favorite
It is cheesy
It is good
I like all macaroni
I put pepper on my macaroni and almost got burned.

At Target

We went down the craft aisle.
First I saw a gallon of glue.
Then I saw magic liquid.
I asked to make slime.
But my Mom said, "No."

Holding a Baby Chicken

Kamrynn Lisenby

· · · ❁ · · ·

I REMEMBER THE FIRST TIME I ever held a baby chicken. I was in second grade. Me and my friends were all in a circle, and the teacher said, "Today we will be holding our chicks!

"Hooray," yelled the class.

I slowly picked up the chicken and it flapped out of my hands and went under my foot.

"Ms. Condon, I almost squished a chicken," I said. I tried to pick up another chick. I heard my friends in the background as I touched a chicken.

McChristian/Giles Family

At the Swimming Pool

Rana McChristian

· · · ✿ · · ·

I REMEMBER SWIMMING IN THAT small backyard pool in Inglewood. I remember getting so dark by the sun....my "tan" lasted well into the start of the school year.

I remember my swim cap popping off of my head. I hated wearing that swim cap my mommy made me wear. She made me put it on every time we would go swimming in Carlo's pool. I did not want to wear it…but I wore it anyway.

I think I look silly in this lavender swim cap, but I wore it anyway. My hair's not gonna get wet, I thought…but I wore it anyway. I convinced myself to wear it because we were only gonna play Marco Polo, and I wouldn't get my hair that wet.

The water is splashing against me…against the sides of the pool. I can hear Earnest and Carlo saying Marco!....Polo!....

I can see the sun, but I must be still in this corner of the pool, so they can't hear me breathe. The water still splashes against my body and, even though I'm quiet, people can still hear that water splashing against wet skin. They can tell someone's in the corner of the pool…even though I'm not saying Marco Polo.

Finally, someone else gets tagged, and IT'S. NOT. ME.

It's summer so the pool games last forever...at least until my swim cap popped off.

I decided to dive into the pool after all. A break from Marco Polo wasn't so bad, and it gave me an opportunity to show off my swimming and aquatic skills. Most of them just know how to play in the pool, I actually know how to swim.

I chose not to run and dive, because the pool is small but I jump in really fast and with great force. The force of that jump and the lavender latex swim cap stretched so tightly over my head… hitting the water was enough to SNAP that swim cap right off my head and land on the ground in the corner where the pool chairs were located.

Everybody laughed, loudly. I was embarrassed. Kids were still laughing, and actually so am I. It was funny and that snapping sound of the latex popping off my head is worth every bit of embarrassment and laughter.

I remember being the only girl in the pool at that time. April and Monique had not come out yet. After all, rushing to swim in a pool with their brothers was nothing new to them, and their mom didn't make them wear caps on their heads.

Rana McChristian

My First Major Scar

Riley Giles

· · · ❀ · · ·

ONE DAY, WHEN MY MOMMY picked me up from kindergarten we were going to the bank. Well, we got to the bank and she had parked the car and was checking her purse to make sure she had what she needed before we went inside. Well, I had already gotten out of the car and I was hopping across the concrete blocks that sit in front of the parking spaces. I was just hopping back and forth on the concrete blocks, then I hopped and tripped over one of the metal bolts that stick out from them. I fell, then slid forward on the black top and got five nasty scrapes up the front of my right shin. They all lined up vertically. I was only five so I was hysterically crying and screaming, while still sitting on the black top holding my leg. *sigh* now we couldn't even go into the bank. She put me back in the car and drove out of the parking lot. Mommy was so mad, she scolded me about how I shouldn't have been hopping on the concrete blocks in the first place and that now she had to make another appointment at the bank. She saw that none of this was helping and that I was still crying and still hysterical so she stopped yelling, got a white towel out of the trunk, pulled over to help me clean up the scar, then took me to Rally's and got me some French Fries!

New Girl on the Block

Riley Giles

· · · ✿ · · ·

IT WAS THE SECOND TO the last day of winter break and I was walking down to the next block over to have a fun in the snow with my friend Olivia. I saw this girl with two fishtail braids down her back, drawing faces in the frost of the window of that yellow house that hadn't been lived in FOR YEARS. I didn't stop to say hi. It was already 4:30 and if I wanted to get through a FULL snowball fight AND build a giant snowman with Olivia, I'd have to speed up!

"Hey!" I called to my friend as I unlatched her gate, while shaking some snow out of my boots. "There's this girl drawing in the window of the yellow house."

Olivia gave me a puzzled look as she smoothed out the edges of a snowball that I could TELL she was ready to hurl at my face.

"You know?! The one that's been on the market since like last October?!"

She flung her arm backwards then *fwwwwmmmmm!!* The cold, icy ball exploded in my face. Then, while I was now shaking snow out of my HAT, she said, "Oh yeah!"

The girl came by later and rested her lilac purple mittens on the fence.

"Hey, in case you were wondering, I live in that yellow house down the street. I'm the new girl on the block!"

Then she ran off, her fishtails blowing in the cold, December wind.

A Bumpy Night

Riley Giles

...⚘...

ON A HOT JUNE AFTERNOON, 1837, I picked cotton on the plantation where my family lived. My family had been planning to run away for quite some time now. My brother Sam had been sold to another plantation in Mississippi a couple of months ago. He wouldn't be able to escape with us, but...he really wanted us to be free.

Later that day, it was about seven o'clock, Master Jenkins' overseer was doing his nightly rounds, checking all the cabins and such. That night, when it was time to run, me, my mama, Mama Rose, my daddy, John, and baby Ester set out on the perilous journey, facing the unforeseen hand of fate to hopefully escape slavery. We made it to the wide creek just outside the woods that concealed the slave plantation from the escape routes. Shoes drenched and all, we crossed the river with ease. We walked barefoot and carried our worn shoes in our hands.

When we reached the first station, an elderly woman came to the door. She spoke no words, but pointed to the back hall closet. We hurried down the long hallway and squeezed into the cramped storage closet. We had been waiting in the darkness for some time when we heard a knock, then a bang, then a bark. The muffled voices of two men talking were TOO familiar. It was the overseer and Master Jenkins' son. I scooted closer to Mama, farther back into the black abyss. Then we heard a click and dogs came stampeding down the long hallway. We could hear their deep, hard breaths, their loud, heavy barks, and their paws padding forcefully on the wooden floor. We pushed aside some clothes on the closet rack. There was a window and we all, one by one, climbed out. Daddy pushed the clothes back and we ran toward the next station.

It was almost morning and all that was in front of us was a large cornfield. We had nowhere to hide, but we couldn't go back to the closet. As the first hint of light rose above the tall cornstalks, we lay on our stomachs and stayed frightfully still. Then we were on our way to the next station, in

Bridgeport, Connecticut. We were far enough now not to have to worry about ever being enslaved for a long time. I was doing this for Sam and all the friends I had on the plantation. Now I'd finally know what it's like to be free.

Stone/Spurlin Family

Links

Lenesha Stone

···✿···

"HA HA HA! OMG! I seen that! Did you see Aunt K face? Wait...it's so loud...Y'all not listening!" I now realize I'm screaming. Cousins surrounding me, aunts on the other side, kids running back and forth. Every two minutes they stop and tell us to watch some new routine they've come up with. We're just sitting here, each trying to come up with the next best thing to say that'll make everyone else laugh. You always know one of those Stone or Mitchell girls will be first on the roster to throw out the first joke against someone else in the room. Our Aunt J will bring up an old memory that still makes her laugh so hard to herself, and we just laugh along.

But it never fails. Aunt D will always be the one who calms down the crowd and says, "Okay, y'all, let's play a game," knowing only about five or six of us will really play because, as soon as she says that, other family's already putting together their #1 spade playing teams.

Once we get started, this can go on for hours. We get to a point that, after so long, we see it's getting dark but we know what that means. That means Mom's gonna say, "Hey, ya'll seen that new comedy show? I've got the DVD. Let's sit and watch it. As we watch, I hear Mom laughing louder than everyone else, while telling them the whole time, "WATCH THIS...Look...HA! Ha! Ha!." In the end, I'm going to laugh. I'm gonna laugh like I didn't just watch this with her two days before. I'm going to laugh until the links never end.

In this room, there are links upon links of love and history that have shaped and made me into who I am today! Without those links, I would have fallen a LONG time ago!

Hot Chocolate

Lenesha Stone

· · · ❁ · · ·

The sun has not risen
But I am up and ready to go
Sunday morning church is what our destination is to be
I have one thing on my mind and church isn't it.

Wearing my favorite pink dress
skipping down the hall in my home
My dad whispering for me to slow down before I wake the others
Same as always, Dad, my brothers, sister and I heading out as quiet as can be.

In the car, anticipation building, but only I know why
Breathing in and out watching the frost from my breath gather in front of me
Dad begging the car heat to hurry up
Driving up Virginia Ave praying my dreams come true

Straight ahead I see "A CASTLE"
Not just any CASTLE, but a HUGE WHITE CASTLE
This castle holds the liquid pleasure that pleases my heart and warms my soul

Finally, we are are at the gate of the castle
One of the sweetest voices I know says
"Good Morning, what can I get for you today?"

Everything within me giggles with excitement to finally hear those two words I dream to hear every Sunday

"Good Morning... May I have FIVE HOT CHOCOLATES please"
At that moment my dreams are now fulfilled

Lenesha Stone

Birthday Persona Poem

Lenesha Stone

· · · ❁ · · ·

Jamaican music playing, thinking back to
My days back on the island.
Today is a day like any other.
Others would usually use this day
To do things I could only dream.
But growing up, birthdays were made into
Just another day like today.
Working, snow everywhere, throwing
Up my hands, yelling, "What's to celebrate,
snow high, what's the fun in that?"
Smokin' my spliff and just wondering.

What Is Your Wild and Precious Life?

Lenesha Stone

· · · ❁ · · ·

Water so blue and clear
you think you can drink it.
I stand here, just now checking into
my hotel of paradise for the first time.
The water goes as far as the eyes can see.
I stand mesmerized by the feel of the air
as it breezes across my face,
sun shining down on me, not being able
to overheat me because it's entangled with
the wonderful breeze from the ocean water.
All I could imagine for myself
at this point is living
in this spot, this exact place forever…

ARUBA, how could life get any better?
The feel of the sand beneath your toes,
breeze from the water,
warmth of the sun…
For life to become any better, I must
continue on my journey to find
what tops this space of the world.
I must find more! I must experience more!

Musik

Lenesha Stone

· · ·⊛· · ·

Foot Stomping, hand clapping, screaming all around
Sitting there barely able to see over the seat in front of me
My body feels heat, it feels like it wants to move but doesn't know what it wants to do
I've seen this scene over and over, Sunday after Sunday

But this time it's different
I don't know what it is but I sit in bewilderment
Fingers slowly tapping on the seat
Head nodding as I continue to watch the show

I know this isn't just a show, there's more to it
But what?
My heart just feels the beat, or does it?
The way these other people are up clapping, jumping, screaming, it has to be more!

I close my eyes and try to feel what this is going on inside of me, hoping it begins to show me how
I should feel.
My body sways, it sways HARD....
I know I've felt this before, here at church, in the car, at home with mom, dad and my siblings
WHAT IS THIS?!?!?!
This feeling, this groove, this BEAT.

MUSIK!

My Cousin Lost

Landon Spurlin

· · · ✿ · · ·

I WAS SAD. MY COUSIN's father died! My cousin was crying and trying to hold the tears. I was sad. I went to my cousin and I said, "I am so sorry," and he said, "It's okay. Let's try to have some fun." And then I went to see his father before he was put in the grave. I was sad. I tried to calm my cousin down. Then I said, "We'll always remember you and we'll always remember him."

I Wish I Was Two Again

I WISH I WAS TWO again. It feels weird to you, but I want to be two again. I want to feel the love. Do you? I hope you do. Anyway, my aunt and me wished I was two and she said, "Ooh, Landon, I wish you were two again." "I do, too," I said. So that is why I want to be two. Thank you. Good night.

My Big Birthday

IT WAS OFF, I WAS sad. I said "I wish somebody remembered my birthday." I opened the door and jumped when I heard the two words I dreamt of, "HAPPY BIRTHDAY." I was happy, I was now six!!! I and my friends partied and I got presents I was very happy. The people said "Happy Birthday, love you."

Hotdogs

Landon Spurlin

· · · ❀ · · ·

WHEN I GO TO THE fair and I am playing, I love to stop and get a hotdog. I ask for hotdogs and I go get them, they are good. I ask for two sometimes and I get ketchup and then I eat them. I eat them fast. I choke but I stop and then eat again and I kick my legs up and down and laughing so hard I fall down and laugh again. I am so happy to eat hotdogs. When I am done I get up and say goodbye and leave. I go play and again get another hotdog and this time I get three hotdogs and I laugh again and again and then play and say goodbye to the hotdogs and I say "see you next year, bye-bye." Next year I go to the fair again. I play and then eat a hotdog. It is so good, it's better than before and I laugh even harder than before and kick up and down even harder and it's so hard that I fall down and my hotdog breaks into two pieces and half falls on the floor. I cry so hard because my other hotdog fell onto the floor and I was really sad and broke into tears right there on the floor and I was really sad so I try and get another hotdog but I am BROKE! I ask my mom for money but my mom only has $2.99. I am doomed, it cost $3.99. I am super doomed.... bye-bye forever

Ray Charles

Landon Spurlin

··· ❀ ···

WHEN I FIRST HEARD RAY Charles it was very good that I was very happy. I said it was magical and I was clapping so hard I could not stop and then stopped and I heard "Let the Good Times Roll" and "Georgia on My Mind" and I felt ready for anything. Georgia on my mind felt peaceful and happy. I love Ray Charles, he is very good, I felt I was him when I first sang his song. I was amazed I felt like I was in sync with him. He is so cool, VERY COOL!! I was going to Asante Children's Theatre because my mommy was a worker with "A.C.T" and I love "A.C.T". I get to do what I love and do what I do best, acting and singing and being funny. I really love Asante Children's Theatre.

Grandpa's Father's Day

IT WAS WEDNESDAY. I WAS alone. I was sitting making a card for Father's Day and it was awesome. I loved the card and a gift for my grandpa. I wanted to say Happy Father's Day.

We were driving to his house and then we were there. I was at the door. My mommy opened the door and I went to make this book. I was so happy to make this book. See you later, bye.

Block Party

Landon Spurlin

· · · ❁ · · ·

I HAD A BLOCK PARTY. It was my sixth birthday party. I was still asleep at 7 a.m. I woke up at 8 a.m. My ma said I was having a party. I was happy. I got dressed and went to my mom's room and said, "What kind of party?" and she said, "Block party." I said, "Yay!"

We got ready for the party and the party started at 1 p.m. It was a good party. I had my daddy and my friends and my brother and it was awesome. I had a blast, but the funny thing was everybody forgot that it's my mom's birthday. Well, all the friends and family never said "Happy birthday, Lenesha" and that made her mad. So me and my mom said it was my mom's birthday and everybody said, "Happy birthday" and then my brother said, "I am staying over for two days," and I was so happy.

When I Am at Home

Landon Spurlin

· · ·❀· · ·

I get home. I have a really tiring day
and a bad day every day. On the weekend
I like to feel like nothing is around me
I sit down, and then when I start to watch TV
I lay down. I feel right to be here
and then I almost fall asleep. I woke myself up
and then I sat up and watched TV
and one time I stayed up until 6 a.m.
I got there at 12 a.m. I got up and said,
"I want to do that every day of the year."

I woke up my mom and said, "I stayed up all night!
I stayed up all night!" and she said, "Wow, Landon,
you stayed up all night. How did you do it?"
And I said, "If I can do it, so can you
and then I walked out of her room
and went to bed and woke up at 6 p.m.
Then I watched TV again till 12 p.m.
Then I said, "Let's do 12:00 to be sure.
I went to bed and then I got an alarm clock
and all was good.

Family Prayer

Landon Spurlin

· · · ❁ · · ·

I get up once every month on Sunday and say
"Mommy, are we going to family prayer?"
And she says, "Yes," and I say, "Yes!"
And then we get ready for it
And we go to family prayer.
I go and play with my cousins
And we play basketball
And they win because they are pros
And because they are in their teens
And then we pray
And then we watch some TV
And then we go home.

My Dad

Leroy Stone

· · · ✿ · · ·

I REMEMBER WHEN MY DAD took me out to teach me how to drive a car. I got behind the wheel. As I was driving my dad made a comment to me throughout the test that I drove better than some adults he knew. Little did he know that my older brother had taken me out for a few test drives, but I dared not tell. I just said, "Thank you, Dad." To this day I am still driving and still striving for perfection.

Washington/Robinson Family

Grandma's House

Vickie Washington

· · · ✿ · · ·

I REMEMBER STANDING IN MY grandma's front yard, the fence was painted white from her paint. The tree trunks were painted white from her paint. There was a mat on the front porch, and a steel chair that she also had painted white using her paint. My oldest memories consist of being at Grandma's house, I have had memories of that front yard since I was a little girl. I remember riding downtown on the bus with Grandma as a little girl. Grandma had a rolling buggy that she used to carry her groceries. I remember there was a Murphy's downtown.

I remember riding the greyhound to Milwaukee with my grandmother. I remember she had a little blue basket or bucket that snapped. She carried our food for the road in it. She would always have some crackers, cheese and Grandma would always fry some chicken that would be soft when we ate it. I remember being in Milwaukee and riding to Wisconsin with Grandma. My Aunt Lora Bee was always there to pick us up. She would always wear a dark blue windbreak every summer. She loved listening to the Carpenters. The house in Milwaukee looked amazing. My aunt's house had a winding stairwell in the back. I loved that. The upstairs of the house, I thought that was so cool. It had a screened-in porch upstairs. My aunt always made pancakes for us. I remember she had an Atari game that was tennis. I would sit on the couch in the living room and play, no noise in the background. I don't remember where everyone was, my aunt may have been upstairs sleep because worked nights. Grandmother was not around much. Maybe she was in another room watching TV, but I don't remember another room downstairs. I remember I slept on a couch that let out into a bed.

I remember leaving Kmart with my first Earth Wind and Fire album, I am not clear which album it was. I just remember being so happy about it because I loved Earth Wind and Fire. I remember riding through Milwaukee with my aunt. I remember they did not listen to a specific radio station.

I remember another time being in Milwaukee, not with Grandma but with the church choir on the church bus. We witnessed a little boy being run over. I remember the bus being pulled over to side of the road. I remember the little boy's mother. I remember it was a bad neighborhood, or the ghetto. That gave me a bad impression of Milwaukee.

I Love You Too Much

Vickie Washington

· · ·❀· · ·

I love you too much, I can't take what you're doing to me.
I can't wait all my life for you to stop being free.

I can't accept you love me and someone else, too.
I want a relationship between us and only us two.

I'm not gonna be #1 with 2 and 3 behind me.
I'm not gonna be #3 with 2 and 1 in front of me.

So make up your mind. If you can't decide,
I see right now I'm wasting my time.

If you're gonna love me, love me true.
Don't love me the way you're loving the other two.

Make up your mind and tell me how you feel.
Once you decide let me know the deal.

I love you so much, I really do.
But not enough to be your fool.

Whatever you decide, I can take it
Whatever happens, I can make it

I'm a strong person and I'm not gonna let you pull me down.
Cause you're not the only person in the word and another love can be found.

Brightwood

Vickie Washington

· · · ✿ · · ·

BETTER KNOWN AS BRIGHTWOOD, THIS neighborhood was filled with families that cared for each other. Many neighbors were responsible for babysitting each other's children, with permission to whip them if necessary. This neighborhood was helpful to one another. Most of the families went to the church down on the corner. The families owned their houses, and when parents died or moved, their children usually took ownership of the houses. Many of the houses are now boarded up or run down, which makes it bad for the houses left behind due to rodents that run wild.

Recipe

Victoria Robinson

· · ·✿· · ·

Ingredients: Marshmallows, Rice Krispies, and butter

1. Melt butter in rusty white flower pot until melted.
2. Have Mommy cut open the bag of marshmallows and dump them in the butter.
3. Take wooden spoon and stir until you tell Mommy "my arms hurt," then she finishes it for you.
4. Add Rice Krispies while Mommy stirs because it's real sticky.
5. Put your creation on the dusted pan cover with foil and put it in the freezer.
6. Sneak in freezer and take some while Mommy isn't looking.
7. Take out freezer and enjoy with Mommy.

The List

1. Be pretty.
2. Be nice.
3. Be classy, don't start no fight.
4. Always be in the shadows because men are afraid you might dim their light.

But me, I don't fit in that list.
Some call me
Loud
Mean
Even a bitch.
But I hold my head up
High and say
I'll just create my own list.

The Man in Our Neighborhood

Victoria Robinson

· · · ❁ · · ·

IT WAS A MAN. ALWAYS on his balcony, standing with a cigarette in his hand. He would always say, "Hi." One day we drove by and he was sitting in a wheelchair with a breather next to him, with a cigarette in his hand. He always said, "Hi." One day he wasn't on the balcony at all. Then we saw his obituary.

WORD DANCE WRITING PROMPTS

Many of the prompts used for WORD DANCE were based on "I Remember," an exercise designed to draw out visual memories. The writer can see the scene in their mind's eye, and further prompts elicit sensory details—taste, touch, smell, and hearing. This exercise can be done individually or in a group. In either case, writers are often surprised to remember things they hadn't thought about in years and by the strong voice and vividness of the stories they write.

I Remember

1. Write "I remember..." and the first memory that comes to mind. Keep doing this for 3-5 minutes, repeating "I remember" each time, writing no more than a phrase or a sentence or two about each memory. Write quickly, don't worry about spelling, punctuation, or the order in which the memories come. (They will be all over the place!) Don't worry about the memories being silly or inconsequential, either. Just remember. Because the flow of memories comes from your right brain, most if not all of the memories will have a visual, even cinematic quality. (Note: Writing "I Remember" every time keeps you in the visual part of the brain. If you make a list instead, it shifts the task to the left brain, which will try to bring order to it too soon.)

2. Count the number of memories you have. Consider each one the first draft of a piece of writing you might develop. Then choose one that you want to write about. (The easiest ones to write about are those that cover a short period of time. For example, instead of writing about a whole summer, write about one experience in the summer. The smaller the time frame is, the more details you can include.)

3. Repeat the "I Remember" exercise with the memory you have chosen, writing down as many details about it as you can remember.

4. Then close your eyes, relax, breathe deeply, and let the scene of your memory come back into your mind. In your mind's eye, look straight ahead. What do you see? Look to the left, to the right. Look down, up, behind you. What do you hear in the scene? What do you smell, taste,

touch? Quickly make a list of all of the additional details you noticed.

5. Freewrite the story of that memory from the picture in your mind's eye, using the details you re-membered (it's okay not to use all of them) and feeling free to add new ones that come into your mind. If you get stuck, look at your list of details and just start writing about any one of them. (Freewrite means exactly what it says: write freely, as fast as you can, with no judgment. Don't worry about spelling, punctuation, organization—any of that. You can always fix that later.)

    NOTE: "Tricks" to jumpstart your freewriting include writing in the present tense, writing the memory as if you're writing it in a letter to someone you love, or writing down the story as if it's a movie playing in your mind.

6. Read your draft. Underline sentences and phrases you like, cross out things that you don't need. Add details that will make the story stronger and clearer.

7. Keep the list of memories you made in the first part of the exercise. You can choose one any time and do the "I Remember" exercise to begin writing about it. You can also do the first part of the exercise again and again. Each time you will probably come up with a whole new list of memories to work with.

This is the story of what happens when...

Finishing this sentence helps you know what the beginning, middle, and end of your story should be. It keeps you focused on showing the reader what happened with scene, detail, and dialogue so that your writing comes alive on the page. Here are a few prompts we used in WORD DANCE.

*   Tell the story of what happened when you lost someone or something you loved.
*   Tell the story of something that happened when you ate your favorite food.
*   Tell the story of something that happened in your neighborhood.
*   Tell the story of what happened when you learned a hard lesson.

Visiting poet Mitchell H.L. Douglas used a variation of this format when he asked WORD DANCE writers to pair up with a family member and tell each other the story of their favorite birthday. Then they wrote each other's stories, as if speaking in their partner's voice—capturing what their partner said, how they said it, and their body language and facial expression as they spoke.

For those who wanted to take another step, Douglas suggested turning what they wrote into a poem. To do that, they should condense the language, add rhythm, and include at least one metaphor or simile for an outward gesture (comparing the content of your poem to something outside of the speaker—and, in the process, implying its connection to the world at large.)

Another World

Visiting speculative fiction writer Maurice Broaddus encouraged WORD DANCE writers to imagine a world and set a story in it. Don't limit your imagination, he said. Ask yourself, What if? Why not? He suggested asking yourself these questions about the imaginary world of your story to help it take form:

- If it's a planet, what is the weather like?
- What are the land and water features? What plants and animals live there? Are there moons?
- If it's an imaginary world on earth, is it new or old?
- What are the neighborhoods like? What people live there? How do they dress, speak, move? What is their religion? How do they spend their days?
- What businesses are there? What institutions?

Fun Forms

Visiting poet Allyson Horton introduced the acrostic poem form, in which you write a word vertically, one letter to a line, then create a sentence or phrase that begins with the first word of each letter. Together the sentences or phrases describe the word in some way. For example, you could write your name and then write a sentence or phrase that describes you for each letter.

She also introduced the list poem, which is simply a list or inventory of items, people, places, things you do, ideas--anything. A list poem can tell a story by listing what happens, line by line, or it can be a list of things that—to the poet—have something in common. A list poem can rhyme, but it doesn't have to. It may use repetition. The important thing is to make the reader think about what is in your list.

Haibun

Visiting poet and co-founder of My Word as Bond Ashley Mack-Jackson introduced haibun, a Japanese form of poetry that combines a prose poem with haiku. The prose poem describes a scene or moment in a way that is rich with sensory details, followed by the haiku in which the poet develops or expands a word or phrase in the prose poem. (A prose poem is written in paragraphs rather than verse, but contains the characteristics of poetry, such as intensity, compactness, rhythm, imagery, and language play. A haiku is three lines with seventeen syllables total: 5-7-5).

Reading Poems

Reading and considering the language and imagery in poems draws out personal memories in a variety of ways. Writers were inspired by these poems:

- Sandra Cisneros's "Good Hot Dogs" inspired WORD DANCE poems about food that reflected Cisneros's use of strong imagery. https://www.youtube.com/watch?v=0usYsgoahuM

- George Ella Lyon's "Where I'm From" provided a model for writing poems that captured the essence of the family members, experiences, and surroundings that shaped the writers' lives. http://www.georgeellalyon.com/where.html

- Mary Oliver's "The Summer Day," with its resonant ending, "Tell me, what is it you plan to do/ with your one wild and precious life?" inspired moving meditations on what matters in life. https://www.loc.gov/poetry/180/133.html

www.ingramcontent.com/pod-product-compliance
Lightning Source LLC
LaVergne TN
LVHW061248060426
835508LV00018B/1544